You and Your
PROBLEMS

BIBLE STUDY GUIDE

From the Bible-teaching ministry of

Charles R. Swindoll

INSIGHT FOR LIVING

Charles R. Swindoll is a graduate of Dallas Theological Seminary and has served in pastorates in Texas, New England, and California since 1963. He has served as senior pastor of the First Evangelical Free Church of Fullerton, California, since 1971. Chuck's radio program, "Insight for Living," began in 1979. In addition to his church and radio ministries, Chuck enjoys writing. He has authored numerous books and booklets on a variety of subjects.

Based on the outlines and transcripts of Chuck's sermons, the study guide text is coauthored by Lee Hough, a graduate of the University of Texas at Arlington and Dallas Theological Seminary. The Living Insights are written by Bill Butterworth, a graduate of Florida Bible College, Dallas Theological Seminary, and Florida Atlantic University.

Editor in Chief:
Cynthia Swindoll

Coauthor of Text:
Lee Hough

Author of Living Insights:
Bill Butterworth

Assistant Editor:
Glenda Schlahta

Copy Manager:
Jac La Tour

Copyediting Supervisor:
Marty Anderson

Copy Editor:
Wendy Peterson

Project Manager:
Alene Cooper

Art Director:
Don Pierce

Designer:
Diana Vasquez

Production Artists:
Gary Lett, Donna Mayo,
and Diana Vasquez

Typographer:
Bob Haskins

Print Production Manager:
Deedee Snyder

Director, Communications Division:
Carla Beck

ISBN 0-8499-8408-4
Printed in the United States of America.
COVER PHOTOGRAPH: The Image Bank/Denny Tillman

CONTENTS

1 Wisdom: An Essential in Handling Problems 1

2 The Problem of Inferiority 10

3 The Problem of the Clergy-Laity Gap 20

4 The Problem of Temptation 26

5 The Problem of Depression 34

6 The Problem of Worry 43

7 The Problem of Anger 50

8 A Cool Hand on a Hot Head 56

9 The Problem of Loneliness 64

10 The Problem of Doubtful Things 71

11 The Problem of Defection 79

12 The Problem of Facing Impossibilities 86

13 The Problem of Death 93

14 Crucial Questions Concerning the Dead 100

15 The Problem of Resentment 108

16 The Problem of Discouragement 115

Books for Probing Further 122

Ordering Information/Order Forms 125

INTRODUCTION

Christians are often criticized for being unrealistic. We're the ones who tend to focus more attention on the positive side of life than the negative . . . the hope of tomorrow instead of the pain of today. Perhaps we are guilty of the charge.

These studies help put things back into proper perspective. They openly admit that we are not immune to many of the same battles that everyone else faces. Problems like anger, depression, inferiority, loneliness, resentment, and other practical difficulties hassle the people of God and therefore need to be addressed.

We are not different because we are free of problems, but because we have a power within us that the world cannot claim—a power that enables us to face the problems which come our way. Hopefully, you will find both realism and encouragement in each of these studies that turn to the Scriptures for counsel that never fails.

Chuck Swindoll

Chuck Swindoll

PUTTING TRUTH INTO ACTION

Knowledge apart from application falls short of God's desire for His children. He wants us to apply what we learn so that we will change and grow. This study guide was prepared with these goals in mind. As you go through the following pages, we hope your desire to discover biblical truth will grow as your understanding of God's Word increases, and that you will be encouraged to apply what you've learned.

To assist you in your study, we've included a section called **Living Insights** at the end of each lesson. These exercises will challenge you to study further and to think of specific ways to put your discoveries into action.

There are many ways to use this guide—in personal devotions, group studies, discussions with friends and family, and Sunday school classes. And, of course, it's an ideal study aid when you're listening to its corresponding "Insight for Living" radio series.

To benefit most from this study guide, we would encourage you to consider it a spiritual journal. That's why we've included space in the **Living Insights** for recording your thoughts and discoveries. We hope you'll return to those sections often for review and encouragement as you continue to grow in your walk with Christ.

Lee Hough
Coauthor of Text

Bill Butterworth
Author of Living Insights

You and Your
PROBLEMS

Chapter 1

WISDOM: AN ESSENTIAL IN HANDLING PROBLEMS

Proverbs 1:1–7, 20–32

Dolores Curran, in *Traits of a Healthy Family*, points out,

> The most common reaction technique of youths in
> conflict with their families is silence. Often silence is
> the only reaction acceptable in the family. If youths
> can't expose what's bothering them for fear of ridicule
> or censure, or if they aren't allowed to argue, then
> they will revert to silence.[1]

Unfortunately, in the larger family of the church, many confused and hurting Christians are also left floundering in a vacuum of silence.

Some have learned that it often isn't safe to openly confess to having too many problems. As one veteran believer observed, "The Christian army is the only one that shoots its own wounded."

Others have been taught that the Christian way to deal with problems is to pray them away—that with enough faith or the right doctrine, we can be free from problems, stress, and disappointment. But when we start believing this line, spirituality starts being measured by our lack of problems instead of our response to them, and we are enticed to equate the goal of eliminating pain with the goal of conformity to Christ.

By applying gradual doses of this teaching, we numb ourselves to the pain we find in reality. We boast about being able to live in

---

1. Dolores Curran, *Traits of a Healthy Family* (Minneapolis, Minn.: Winston Press, 1983), p. 44.

1

the boiling waters of this world without getting scalded. But beneath the calloused layers of denial are problems painful to the touch.

In this series dealing with *You and Your Problems*, we'll explore the biblical view of problems and how God wants us to approach them.

Principles about Problems

Let's begin our study by inoculating our thinking with four basic principles.

First: *It is incorrect to think that once you become a Christian, all your problems will be solved.* Jesus is often peddled as a panacea for eliminating problems: "Come to Christ and all your problems will be solved!" Yet the Bible never says this, and we do a disservice to people when we tell them He does.

Second: *It is incorrect to say that all problems are discussed in the Bible.* Far more problems than we think are specifically discussed in its pages, but too often we attempt to speak authoritatively on issues the Bible does not address.

Third: *It is incorrect to believe that having problems is a sign of spiritual immaturity.* Spirituality is not measured by the number of problems a person has or doesn't have. Problems are an inseparable part of being human in an aching, fallen world—we all experience them, just as Job, Paul, Peter, and the disciples did.

Fourth: *It is incorrect to assume that exposure to biblical instruction alone will result in the removal of your problems.* It is one thing to grow *old* in the Lord. It's another thing to grow *up* in the Lord. Many people faithfully attend churches, Sunday schools, and Bible conferences for years, hoarding up the great truths of the faith in worn notebooks and impressive libraries. Yet they still exhibit behavior that is inconsistent with all their knowledge. Remember what Jesus said in Matthew 7?

> "Therefore everyone who hears these words of Mine, and *acts* upon them, may be compared to a wise man, who built his house upon the rock. And the rain descended, and the floods came, and the winds blew, and burst against that house; and yet it did not fall, for it had been founded upon the rock. And everyone who hears these words of Mine, and does not act upon them, will be like a foolish man, who built his house upon the sand. And the rain descended, and the floods came, and the winds blew, and burst against that house; and it fell, and great was its fall." (vv. 24–27, emphasis added)

2

Both builders heard Jesus' words, but only one put them into practice. Exposure to God's Word does not in itself produce maturity. It will not solve one problem until we begin applying it.

Problems and Proverbs

Someone has said that the book of Psalms teaches us how to get along with God, while Proverbs teaches us how to get along with people. Psalms helps us in our devotional life, while Proverbs helps us in our practical life. Psalms brings us into the heavenlies, while Proverbs sets our feet in the grass roots of human life.

Most of Proverbs is written by Solomon, the wisest man who ever lived. He enjoyed great material wealth and a rich spiritual heritage, which was passed on to him from his father, King David. His advice on daily living is the practical advice of someone who struggled with problems—just as we do. In Proverbs, Solomon opens the doors to his greatest treasure chamber, sharing with us the priceless wisdom God has given to him.

Solomon begins his book by listing the benefits of studying these proverbs.

> The proverbs of Solomon the son of David, king
> of Israel:
> To know wisdom and instruction,
> To discern the sayings of understanding,
> To receive instruction in wise behavior,
> Righteousness, justice and equity;
> To give prudence to the naive,
> To the youth knowledge and discretion.
> (Prov. 1:1–4)

The first benefit of studying Proverbs is that we'll "know wisdom and instruction." Wisdom is looking at life from God's point of view.

The second benefit is that we will learn to "discern the sayings of understanding." If wisdom is *looking* at life from God's viewpoint, understanding is *responding* to life from God's viewpoint.

The third benefit is that we will "receive instruction in wise behavior, righteousness, justice, and equity." The term *receive* suggests action or mobility. It's the term associated with "plucking grapes and taking them with you." In this instance, it refers to instruction that is to be plucked and taken like succulent fruit from a vine.

The fourth benefit is that we'll gain "prudence," "knowledge," and "discretion." Notice that Solomon specifically includes *the youth*

3

in this benefit (v. 4b). How many times, as you were growing up, can you remember hearing those squelching words, "You're not old enough!" Solomon, however, puts no age limit on who can benefit from the study of this book.

Young people today are constantly bombarded with the world's wisdom—why not give them some wisdom from God's Word? Companies exist whose sole purpose is to study young people so that they can manipulate what they will eat, drink, wear, think, and do. And the media, on which so many of our children are being raised, is not exactly scriptural when it comes to values. We must not only encourage our young people to learn the wisdom of Proverbs, we must model it ourselves.

General Observations about Wisdom

Toward the end of chapter 1, Solomon takes the abstract principle of wisdom and turns it into a person, a woman who cries out in the noisy thoroughfares of life. Before we walk past her, lost in our own thoughts, let's lift our heads to hear her voice. From what she says, we can make three important observations.

Wisdom is available.

Wisdom shouts in the street,
She lifts her voice in the square;
At the head of the noisy streets she cries out;
At the entrance of the gates in the city, she utters her
    sayings: . . .
"Turn to my reproof,
Behold, I will pour out my spirit on you;
I will make my words known to you."
(vv. 20–21, 23)

God didn't empty His supply of wisdom on Solomon. It is still available to us every time we open our Bibles.

Wisdom can be spurned.

"I called, and you refused;
I stretched out my hand, and no one paid attention;
And you neglected all my counsel,
And did not want my reproof."
(vv. 24–25)

Our problem is not exposure to wisdom—our problem is experiencing it. We march by wisdom's outstretched hand every day, tossing a careless "No, thank you" over our shoulders as we crane our necks to find something more exciting.

When wisdom is rejected, the results are always bitter.

We may casually cast wisdom aside, but the consequences are anything but casual. Verses 26–32 describe what happens when we hear wisdom's voice and reject it.

"I will even laugh at your calamity;
I will mock when your dread comes,
When your dread comes like a storm,
And your calamity comes on like a whirlwind,
When distress and anguish come on you.
Then they will call on me, but I will not answer;
They will seek me diligently, but they shall not find me,
Because they hated knowledge,
And did not choose the fear of the Lord.
They would not accept my counsel,
They spurned all my reproof.
So they shall eat of the fruit of their own way,
And be satiated with their own devices.
For the waywardness of the naive shall kill them,
And the complacency of fools shall destroy them."

When we've rejected wisdom's healthy counsel week after week, month after month, year after year and gorged ourselves on the world's artificially sweet advice, we can expect to experience some discomfort. But God doesn't offer any panic packages of wisdom that can plop-plop-fizz-fizz our problems away. It'll take a careful new diet and strenuous exercise to shape up those sour situations and distorted values.

Profiling Those Who Spurn Wisdom

Verse 22 labels three types of people whose common characteristic is the refusal of wisdom.

"How long, O naive ones, will you love simplicity?
And scoffers delight themselves in scoffing,
And fools hate knowledge?"

The Simple

The word *naive* or *simple* carries the idea of a "wide open door." The simple person is wide open, easily influenced, gullible. This person lacks discernment, becoming an easy target for someone such as the harlot described in chapter 7. The simple are easily enticed because they lack understanding and are therefore unaware of danger.

Solomon tells us in 22:3 that the simple also never learn from their mistakes. The original Hebrew conveys the idea that they are making the same mistakes today that they were five years ago and will be making five years from now.

Proverbs 1:4a adds one further insight: without prudence the simple are unable to look beyond the surface of things to see what's really there. They are easily enchanted by the music of pied pipers, following them wherever they're going without question.

The Scoffer

The word *scoff* means "to turn aside, to mock, to reject with vigorous contempt, to refuse, to show disdain, to be disgusted." Scoffers don't simply agree to disagree; they seem driven to scorn and ridicule anything that opposes their ideas. Wisdom warns us against our natural impulses when dealing with these kinds of people.

> He who corrects a scoffer gets dishonor for himself,
> And he who reproves a wicked man gets insults for
> himself.
> Do not reprove a scoffer, lest he hate you,
> Reprove a wise man, and he will love you.
> (9:7–8)

No amount of counseling will change this person's attitude. No amount of exposure to biblical truth will penetrate this person's thick crust of skepticism (see 14:6).

The Fool

Typically, when we think of the word *fool* we picture someone who lacks intelligence. But the biblical meaning of *fool* is "not so much one lacking in mental powers, as one who misuses them; not one who does not reason, but reasons wrongly."[2] No greater example can be found than by comparing Psalm 14:1a, which says:

> The fool has said in his heart, "There is no God,"

to Proverbs 1:7:

> The fear of the Lord is the beginning of knowledge;
> Fools despise wisdom and instruction.

The word *fool* also carries with it the connotation of wickedness.

---

2. Merrill F. Unger, *Unger's Bible Dictionary*, 3d ed., rev. (Chicago, Ill.: Moody Press, 1966), p. 375.

Imitating One Who Embraces Wisdom

Now that we've explored three types of people who reject wisdom, let's look at someone who embraces it. Of the 186 different characters Solomon uses to parade wisdom's truths in the book of Proverbs, one stands out above the rest. This is the "wise man," who is first mentioned in verse 5:

> A wise man will hear and increase in learning,
> And a man of understanding will acquire wise counsel.

If we take a moment to study this verse, we'll see that at least three traits characterize wise people.

First: *Wise people are willing listeners* (see also 12:15, 13:1, 15:31–32, 19:20). Solomon begins with hearing, but sadly, this is often last on the list for many people today, as Paul Tournier affirms:

> Listen to all the conversations of our world, those between nations as well as those between couples. They are for the most part dialogues of the deaf. Each one speaks primarily in order to set forth his own ideas, in order to justify himself, in order to enhance himself and to accuse others.[3]

Solomon says, "A wise man will hear."

Second: *Wise people desire to learn and grow* (see also 9:9, 10:14). Too often in our culture we concentrate all our learning in our school years and figure we're through with it when we graduate. But this should not be the case. Learning new things and expanding the horizons of our minds should be a lifelong pursuit. Solomon says, "Increase in learning."

Third: *Wise people eagerly seek out and accept wise counsel* (see also 12:15, 13:10). Rather than taking an I-can-do-it-myself attitude, wise people realize that they don't know everything and take to heart Solomon's advice in 11:14—

> Where there is no guidance, the people fall,
> But in abundance of counselors there is victory.

They don't take just anybody's advice, however; they exercise discernment and seek out "wise counsel."

Through the daily application of wisdom's principles, we, too, can become mature, wise people.

3. Paul Tournier, *To Understand Each Other*, trans. John S. Gilmour (Atlanta, Ga.: John Knox Press, 1967), pp. 8–9.

Problems, Wisdom, and Us

All of us are in need of regular attitudinal checkups. Before wisdom can enter our hearts, before any problem can be solved, simplicity, scoffing, and foolishness must be dealt with. Once these are put away, then we can begin the practice of applying the balm of God's wisdom to the problems we face. The regular application of wisdom to our lives can serve as an effective preventative for many of the common ills that beset us.

🍇 *Living Insights* STUDY ONE

A study of *You and Your Problems* sounds kind of intimidating, doesn't it? But that's only because we're seeing our problems from an earthbound perspective. What we want to do in this series is to explore these problems from God's perspective, to learn to look at life from His point of view. Which, in essence, is what wisdom is. And there's no better place to learn about wisdom than in the book written by the wisest man who ever lived.

* Beginning with the first chapter, read as much of the book of Proverbs as your time allows. Pay special attention to the statements Solomon makes about wisdom, and write down your observations in the following chart.

Wisdom

Reference	Observations

"Acquire wisdom! Acquire understanding!" Solomon exhorts in Proverbs 4:5a. But as we saw in our lesson, not everyone is willing to follow this advice. How about you? Are you willing to take his words to heart? Or are you being held back by a part of yourself that prefers to remain simple, scoffing, or foolish? Rather than condemning yourself or getting defensive, use this exercise to pinpoint these troublesome areas of your life and bring them before the Lord.

* In what ways do you find yourself identifying with the description of the simple person?

_____

_____

* The scoffer?

_____

_____

* The fool?

_____

_____

If you are discouraged by what you've found, don't be! When we face our shortcomings, our forgiving Lord is always faithful to give us a fresh start.

> But if any of you lacks wisdom, let him ask of God,
> who gives to all men generously and without reproach,
> and it will be given to him. (James 1:5)

How's that for help and hope in facing your problems?

Chapter 2

THE PROBLEM OF INFERIORITY

Selected Scripture

P erhaps there is no better picture of inferiority than the one seen in the following note, written by a seven-year-old boy to a psychotherapist who works with children:

> Dear Docter Gardner
>
> What is bothering me is that long ago some big person it was a boy about 13 years old. He called me turtle and I know he said that because of my plastic sergery.
>
> And I think god hates me because of my lip. And when I die he'll probably send me to hell.
>
> Love, Chris[1]

If we could squeeze Chris' note between our hands, we would probably extract the bitter juices of feelings we have had ourselves. Feelings such as a deep sense of unworthiness, acute inadequacy, lack of confidence, and an inability to accept ourselves.

Inferiority is a parasite of sin that feeds off our separation from God. It first became attached to mankind through that act of rebellion in the Garden, and since then, it has gorged itself on the unstable substitutes for God that people rely on for worthiness.

In today's market, the commodities of beauty, intelligence, and wealth pay the highest dividends of conferred worth. Without them, we are made to feel we are something less than we should be. We are harangued daily by society's built-in slant that rewards the haves and punishes the have-nots. In this brutal cultural milieu of the survival of the worthiest, the less gifted attempt to survive by trying to compensate through overachievement, superiority complexes, and sarcasm. Yet, despite our best efforts to clothe ourselves with worth, underneath it all the parasite of inferiority still feeds on our souls.

And just because we are Christians does not mean that we're automatically excused from the self-mutilating feelings of inferiority.

---

1. As quoted by James Dobson, in *Hide or Seek*, rev. ed. (Old Tappan, N.J.: Fleming H. Revell Co., 1979), p. 58.

Too often we have also felt them cut into our thoughts and drain the life out of our spirits.

In this lesson we'll turn to the timeless counsel of the Bible and reach for God's help in dealing with the painful problem of inferiority.

Biblical Illustrations

For the next few moments, let's go back in time and look at three men of the Bible: two who struggled greatly with inferiority, and one who should have—by the world's standards—but didn't.

Moses

When we come across Moses in Exodus 3, we see a man whose background is littered with failure. Having murdered a man (see 2:11–14), been exiled from the opulence of Egypt to the sparseness of the Midian desert (see v. 15), and lived in obscurity for the past forty years herding sheep, Moses is probably besieged by feelings of inferiority brought on by guilt over these failures.

But despite Moses' feelings of worthlessness, God still wants to use him. Getting his attention through a burning bush, the Lord speaks to Moses and commissions him to free Israel.

> "And now, behold, the cry of the sons of Israel has come to Me; furthermore, I have seen the oppression with which the Egyptians are oppressing them. There-fore, come now, and I will send you to Pharaoh, so that you may bring My people, the sons of Israel, out of Egypt." (3:9–10)

God has given him great news! But all Moses hears is *"I will send you."* And from this moment on, he has difficulty getting off the train of thought that travels only through his inadequacies—flashes of past failures providing his only scenery.

> But Moses said to God, "Who am I, that I should go to Pharaoh, and that I should bring the sons of Israel out of Egypt?" (v. 11)

Sounds like a humble response, doesn't it? But it's not. As Chris-tian counselor Gary Collins says, "Humility involves a grateful de-pendence on God and a realistic appraisal of both our strengths and weaknesses."[2] From this and the rest of Moses' responses, we can

---

2. Gary R. Collins, *Christian Counseling: A Comprehensive Guide* (Waco, Tex.: Word Books, 1980), p. 349.

see that self-doubt has narrowed his vision to the point that he can focus only on himself and not on the One who speaks with him.

Just look at his conversation with God: God promises His *presence* (v. 12)—but Moses responds, "What if they don't believe me?" (4:1). God promises His *power* (vv. 2–9)—but Moses responds, "But I'm not real good with words" (v. 10). God assures him of His *plan* (v. 12)—but Moses responds, "Please Lord, get a substitute" (v. 13).

Moses vividly mirrors the truth that how we view ourselves will affect how we interpret everything around us. It explains how we may look straight into the brilliance of the morning sun and see only darkness; how God's fiery presence was only inches away, yet all Moses could see was the blackness of his own inadequacies.

Jeremiah

Now let's look over Jeremiah's shoulder in the first chapter of his book. In the few seconds it will take to flip over to this passage, eight hundred years will have passed since Moses' day. Here God again wants to recruit a man into His service.

> Now the word of the Lord came to me saying,
> "Before I formed you in the womb I knew
>   you,
> And before you were born I consecrated
>   you;
> I have appointed you a prophet to the
>   nations."
> (Jer. 1:4–5)

But, like Moses, Jeremiah also responds with inferiority instead of humility.

> Then I said, "Alas, Lord God!
> Behold, I do not know how to speak,
> Because I am a youth." (v. 6)

Do Jeremiah's and Moses' excuses remind you of your own? "Love my enemies, Lord? Gee, I don't know—you see I'm not the best at . . ." "Pray, Lord? Well, I'm not any good at talking. If only I had . . . If it weren't for . . ." These familiar refrains have eulogized low self-esteem for centuries.

Amos

Before leaving this scrapbook of Old Testament figures, let's look at the less familiar face of Amos—someone whose faith guarded him against inferiority's touch. If we were to measure his worth by the world's standards, the indicator would probably drop down below "needs improvement" to "loser." He has had no formal education, and he isn't attractive or eloquent. He is a simple fig picker by occupation—he harvests fruit from sycamore trees. And to top it all off, he has stained hands from mashing the fruit to make it soft for the buyer—some prophet of God! Nevertheless, he is the man God chooses to represent Him before Amaziah, the priest of Bethel. When the socially polished, beautifully attired, eloquent, and unsaved priest hears what Amos has to say, he tells him, in no uncertain terms, to get out.

> Then Amaziah said to Amos, "Go, you seer, flee away
> to the land of Judah, and there eat bread and there
> do your prophesying!" (Amos 7:12)

However, Amos doesn't back away. He doesn't look down at his clothes or his stained hands and wonder what in the world he is doing there. Instead, he keeps his eyes focused on the Lord; he stands firm on the truths God has revealed to him and refuses to leave until Amaziah hears them all.

> Then Amos answered and said to Amaziah, "I am
> not a prophet, nor am I the son of a prophet; for I am
> a herdsman and a grower of sycamore figs. But the
> Lord took me from following the flock and the Lord
> said to me, 'Go prophesy to My people Israel.'"
> (vv. 14–15)

Amos demonstrates how the Lord can transform people who will keep their eyes focused on Him. It *is* possible for us to be freed from the bondage of measuring our worth by the fluctuating values of the world market.

Personal Insights

Now that we've seen the problem of inferiority illustrated in the lives of Moses, Jeremiah, and Amos, let's turn to the New Testament and see what principles we can learn from their lives.

The Lord's Estimate of You

In Matthew 6 Jesus shares a profound truth that can dispel our dark clouds of self-doubt.

> "Look at the birds of the air, that they do not sow,
> neither do they reap, nor gather into barns, and yet
> your heavenly Father feeds them. Are you not worth
> much more than they?" (v. 26)

Even though the subject of this verse is worry, the point made about our value cannot be missed. If God is concerned about the little birds in the sky, will He not be all the more concerned about you (see also 10:29–31)? God loves you to the immeasurable extent of sacrificing His Son. Can any greater value be bestowed on your life?

Your Worth in the Body

The body of Christ is the entire family of God on earth today. Every living soul, around the world, who is a born-again believer in Christ is a member of His body. Christ is the Head of this body, and the rest of us, as Paul explains in 1 Corinthians 12, are fingers, arms, knees, toes, or even tiny organs that are rarely seen. However, instead of being content to be the parts God has designed us to be, we invite inferiority to creep in as we compare ourselves to each other.

> For the body is not one member, but many. If the foot should say, "Because I am not a hand, I am not a part of the body," it is not for this reason any the less a part of the body. And if the ear should say, "Because I am not an eye, I am not a part of the body," it is not for this reason any the less a part of the body. If the whole body were an eye, where would the hearing be? If the whole were hearing, where would the sense of smell be? (vv. 14–17)

When the eye wants to become an ear, when the foot decides that what it really wants to be is a nose, when the thumb wants to become an elbow; we put more value on who we think we should be and less on who God wants us to be, and the body cannot function. But in verses 18–25, God tells us that He has placed each of us where He wants us—that all the parts of the body, seen or unseen, are essential and share an equal value.

Your Estimate of You

> For through the grace given to me I say to every man among you not to think more highly of himself than he ought to think; but to think so as to have sound judgment, as God has allotted to each a measure of faith. (Rom. 12:3)

With pride as our teacher, we become arrogant and our sense of worth gets overinflated. Under inferiority's tutelage, we belittle ourselves into thinking we're insignificant to God and other people. But Paul exhorts us to have a sane or "sound" estimate of ourselves. And we can have such an estimate *only* as we accept God's view of us.

14

Pulling all this together, we can draw out four statements of application.

First: *Realize you were prescribed before birth.* Realize that God made you. You are not just a product of chance, but rather a work of art from the mind of God. He has placed His signature on you with the indelible ink of His image. Nothing about you or the days of your life—even before you had taken your first breath—has escaped the loving scrutiny of your heavenly Father.

> For Thou didst form my inward parts;
> Thou didst weave me in my mother's womb.
> I will give thanks to Thee, for I am fearfully and
>   wonderfully made;
> Wonderful are Thy works,
> And my soul knows it very well.
> My frame was not hidden from Thee,
> When I was made in secret,
> And skillfully wrought in the depths of the earth.
> Thine eyes have seen my unformed substance;
> And in Thy book they were all written,
> The days that were ordained for me,
> When as yet there was not one of them.
> (Ps. 139:13–16)

Second: *Remember that the growth process is still going on.* At times we become frustrated with our slow growth and open the door to self-defeat: "I'm no good . . . I keep making the same mistakes . . . God is probably sick of me." But Paul tells us, "Hold on. Get your eyes off of yourself, and stay confident in the fact that God is at work in you—even when you don't see it."

> For I am confident of this very thing, that He who
> began a good work in you will perfect it until the day
> of Christ Jesus. (Phil. 1:6)

Third: *Refuse to compare yourself with others.* Second Corinthians 10:5b states: "We are taking every thought captive to the obedience of Christ." Our feelings of inferiority thrive on those renegade thoughts we allow to pass through our minds uncontested. They can run by so quickly sometimes that we are not even aware of thinking them. To get control of them, we must train ourselves to constantly stand guard at the door of our minds with the truth. Inferiority never rests. It will seize every opportunity we give it to continue brain-washing us with its doctrine of worthlessness. It boils down to this: Will you submit to the liberating truth of Christ, or will you submit to being held prisoner to the lies of inferiority?

15

Fourth: *Respond correctly to your shortcomings.* We all have defects, scars, or shortcomings that we must learn to deal with. Paul provides us with a personal glimpse in 2 Corinthians 12:7–9 into how he handled one such problem.

> And because of the surpassing greatness of the revelations, for this reason, to keep me from exalting myself, there was given me a thorn in the flesh, a messenger of Satan to buffet me—to keep me from exalting myself! Concerning this I entreated the Lord three times that it might depart from me. And He has said to me, "My grace is sufficient for you, for power is perfected in weakness." Most gladly, therefore, I will rather boast about my weaknesses, that the power of Christ may dwell in me.

From this we can discern three things: first, we can feel the freedom to pray to have these things corrected. Second, if the Lord chooses to leave them with us, we must learn to accept our shortcomings as a way for God to display His power in and through us. Third, Paul points out that the news of shortcomings is not all bad. For it is often in our areas of weakness that we see most clearly the reality of the Savior's work in our lives.

Feelings of inferiority that have built up over the years are difficult to overcome. But it can be done! We must resist the pull to place our self-worth, and the worth of others, in the same values the world buys stock in. To do this, we must follow God's advice in Romans 12:2 to renew our minds in His truth. As members of the body of Christ, we must help one another sensitively and faithfully apply the God-provided truths about our worth.

Living Insights

Most of us struggle with inadequacy, yet we cover it up so well that it may not be detectable even to those who are closest to us. To get a handle on this painful problem, let's look at how our relationship with God can be vital in validating our worth. After reading the following statements, look up the verses and summarize what they say.

• Because of our relationship with God the Father, we can know we are accepted and feel that we belong.

16

Matthew 10:29–31 _____

_____

Romans 8:15–17 _____

_____

Ephesians 1:3–6 _____

_____

- Because of our relationship with the Son of God, we can know feelings of worth.

  John 1:12–13 _____

  _____

  John 10:27–30 _____

  _____

  Romans 5:6–8 _____

  _____

  Romans 8:35–39 _____

  _____

- Because of our relationship with the Holy Spirit, we can be assured of competence.

  John 14:16–17, 26 _____

  _____

  _____

John 16:13–15 _____

_____

_____

Romans 8:26–27 _____

_____

_____

🍇 *Living Insights*

Oftentimes we can better focus our thoughts by putting them on paper. Let's do that with this topic of inferiority.

• Under each practical suggestion, write a paragraph from your heart. Include your true feelings about how these statements relate or don't relate to your life. Conclude by lifting your thoughts to God in prayer.

1. Realize you were prescribed before birth. _____

_____

_____

_____

_____

2. Remember that the growth process is still going on._____

_____

_____

_____

_____

3. Refuse to compare yourself to others. _____

_____

_____

_____

_____

4. Respond correctly to your shortcomings. _____

_____

_____

_____

_____

Chapter 3

THE PROBLEM OF THE CLERGY-LAITY GAP

1 Thessalonians 2:1–12

The greatest wall ever built by human hands stretches 1500 miles along the northern boundary of China. It was begun in the third century B.C. by the emperor Shih Huang Ti in defense against the Huns, who threatened to invade.

The largest wall ever built by living creatures is the Great Barrier Reef off the northeastern coast of Australia. Extending 1250 miles, the reef has been built up through the centuries with "bricks" made from the skeletons and remains of marine animals and organisms.

The deepest gap ever carved out of nature is the Grand Canyon, which ranges from 4 to 18 miles wide and 5300 feet deep. It has been gouged out over time primarily by the Colorado River, which erodes more than half a million tons of sediment a day.

Walls. Barriers. Gaps. They all do the same thing—divide. But the most imposing divisions mankind will ever know are the invisible ones . . . and you and I are their architects.

Brick by brick, with each sharp word that wounds us, we erect a barrier, we build a wall. And with each painful encounter, our relationships erode and a gap is formed, separating us from each other.

Relational barriers exist not only between individuals, but also between groups of people. For example, for many centuries an ecclesiastical wall separated the clergy from the laity. And it happens today too. Whenever the pastor puts himself on a pedestal or when he is put there by the people, a gap yawns between them. Clergy as well as laity must work together to keep a gap between the pulpit and the pew from opening.

Paul's Philosophy regarding His Ministry

One clergyman who successfully kept relational gaps from developing was the apostle Paul. In a letter to the Thessalonian believers, he wrote,

> For you yourselves know, brethren, that our coming to you was not in vain. (1 Thess. 2:1)

It was as if he was saying, "As I look back on our time in Thessalonica, I see it not as a worthless time, not as something that caused a big gap to come between us." Instead, the time was marked by great fellowship and a heart-to-heart love for one another. How did Paul keep barriers out of his ministry, the walls down between himself and the folks in the pew? In verses 3–9 he recalls six distinguishing marks of his ministry that can help us prevent gaps from forming today.

His exhortation was based on truth, not deceit.

> For our exhortation does not come from error or impurity or by way of deceit. (v. 3)

Because Paul's ministry was based on truth, the Thessalonians could trust him—they didn't need to question his motives and wonder, Why is he really saying that? By building trust and confidence through his openness and honesty, Paul was able to form an intimate relationship with these believers, which is seen in his choice of the word *exhortation*. The Greek root for this term means "to call alongside." It conveys the idea of a friend coming close to encourage and comfort—and when necessary, to confront. Not in a hammering, badgering, or buffeting way; but simply telling the truth in love . . . from one friend to another.

His message glorified God, not man.

> But just as we have been approved by God to be entrusted with the gospel, so we speak, not as pleasing men but God, who examines our hearts. For we never came with flattering speech, as you know, nor with a pretext for greed—God is witness—nor did we seek glory from men, either from you or from others. (vv. 4–6a)

Paul could have created a gap if he'd come to glorify himself or anyone other than God. But as a trusted bond servant of the One who had sent him, he desired only to faithfully communicate his Master's message. For he knew, when God called him from the Damascus road and sent him to the Arabian Desert, that his mission was prescribed by God. Therefore, he was determined to see that God alone would be pleased and glorified.

His ministry was one of tenderness, not force.

> As apostles of Christ we might have asserted our authority. But we proved to be gentle among you, as a nursing mother tenderly cares for her own children. (vv. 6b–7)

21

If any man had the right to assert his authority, it was Paul. After all, he was an apostle. He was a powerful man. He could have chosen to misuse his power and build himself an empire . . . to control others with a demanding attitude. But he chose the selfless role of a "nursing mother" instead, yearning to meet the needs of God's children in Thessalonica with a tender attitude of humility.

He shared his life, not just his words.

> Having thus a fond affection for you, we were well-pleased to impart to you not only the gospel of God but also our own lives, because you had become very dear to us. (v. 8)

The word *impart* means "to give a share of something." To Paul, the Thessalonians were not simply another audience for him to lecture to and then move on. He stayed with them and fleshed out the gospel he preached. His whole life incarnated God's love and redemption in Jesus Christ.

Ministry isn't lobbing instructions from the sidelines to those who are struggling in the game of life. It's laying aside the clerical robes and donning sweatpants and tennis shoes to join the rest of the players.

His labor was based on dedication, not money.

> For you recall, brethren, our labor and hardship, how working night and day so as not to be a burden to any of you, we proclaimed to you the gospel of God. (v. 9)

Paul never failed to remember his calling. He was dedicated to it, for the calling was from God and not of his own making. Motivation for ministry must always come from dedication, not from selfish gain.

His example was positive and encouraging, not negative and critical.

> You are witnesses, and so is God, how devoutly and uprightly and blamelessly we behaved toward you believers; just as you know how we were exhorting and encouraging and imploring each one of you as a father would his own children. (vv. 10–11)

Paul acted toward the Thessalonians as a father would toward his own children. He was devoted to them, treating them in an upright and blameless way.

Many studies have affirmed the truth conveyed by Paul's imagery of a leader being like a parent, in that parents are primarily responsible for the general mood of the home—their positive spirit breeds harmony and happiness and creates delight. Negative, critical parents, however, invariably create a wall between themselves and their children—just as a negative, critical minister creates a gap between himself and the flock God has called him to serve.

Paul's Goal regarding His Ministry

In verse 12 Paul explains what his goal was in working with the believers at Thessalonica:

> That you may walk in a manner worthy of the God who calls you into His own kingdom and glory.

Paul believed that a minister should reach out, equipping his flock to have a lifestyle that's "worthy of the God who calls [them]." And apparently, his heartfelt concerns were well received. The Thessalonian assembly was known throughout Greece and Macedonia as a church who modeled great faith toward God and endurance in times of suffering (1:7, 2:14).

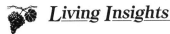 *Living Insights* STUDY ONE

We've just looked—from the pastor's perspective—at ways to keep gaps from forming between pastors and their congregations. But pastors are not the only ones who should be concerned with "gap-control." Let's use our time today to see how well we're doing at building bridges instead of barriers.

- Paul's philosophy of ministry had six directives undergirding it, which we have summarized for you from the perspective of a layperson. In the following chart, put a check (✔) beside the answer that best evaluates your success in the gap-prevention process.

Continued on next page

My Success in Preventing Gaps			
Summary Statement	Doing Well	Needs Work	Don't Ask
I am truthful and transparent with my pastor.	☐	☐	☐
I glorify God instead of my pastor.	☐	☐	☐
I have a tender attitude of humility, rather than a controlling or demanding one.	☐	☐	☐
I share my life with those who lead me.	☐	☐	☐
I am dedicated to God, not selfish gain.	☐	☐	☐
I try to be positive and encouraging, not negative or critical.	☐	☐	☐

- Did you find an area in which you might be contributing to a clergy-laity gap? If you did, take time now to write out a strategy to begin bridging that gap.

_____

_____

_____

_____

_____

_____

_____

_____

Living Insights   STUDY TWO

Paul had fond memories of his time with the Thessalonians. Will your pastor or Sunday school teacher have similar feelings when looking back over the time spent leading your congregation or class?

- Can you think of some specific ways to deepen your relationship with your minister or teacher? Maybe a note, or perhaps a card, gift, or phone call. Are you gifted in a way that could prove helpful? Plan some ways to make warm memories for your leader this week.

_____

_____

_____

_____

_____

_____

_____

_____

_____

Chapter 4

THE PROBLEM
OF TEMPTATION

James 1:13–15

M ark Antony was known as the silver-throated orator of Rome.
He was also credited with being a brilliant man, a strong leader,
and a courageous soldier . . . but one thing he lacked was strength of
character. On the outside, he was impressive and magnificent—but
on the inside, he was weak and vulnerable. This so enraged his tutor
that on one occasion he shouted at him, "O Marcus! O colossal child
. . . able to conquer the world but unable to resist a temptation!"

That indictment fits not only Mark Antony but also many of us
today. No one is immune to the bewitching appeals of temptation's
sirens. And some, like Antony, find it virtually impossible to resist
the pull of their alluring voices.

As we enter into this study on temptation, we must keep in mind
that there are other temptations besides sensual ones. When we
focus all our attention on guarding against sexual temptation, we
provide easy access to the hordes of other temptations waiting to
sneak in behind our backs . . . like the temptation to gossip, to
envy, to love money, to judge someone unfairly, or to be selfish.
Temptation's legions constantly test the strength of our inner forti-
tude. They bombard us with grenades of vanity, rocket fire of flattery,
and fusillades of enticements. All for the purpose of leading our wills
captive, away from God.

The Difference between Trials and Temptation

To begin, let's turn to the book of James, a letter written to the
Christian Jews scattered throughout the ancient world (James 1:1).
Isolated from the wellsprings of a warm and supportive Christian
community, these people needed James' practical advice on trials
and temptation.

Trials

James begins his letter by addressing the problem of trials. It is
important to understand that a trial is an ordeal; it's a hardship,
something that puts our faith to the test.

26

Many people think that the presence of trials indicates the presence of sin, but nothing could be further from the truth. There is nothing inherently immoral or sinful about experiencing a trial, as we can see from the lives of a few well-known Bible figures. Job, for example, faced excruciating losses in practically every area of his life (Job 1–2). Elijah experienced deep depression when his life was threatened (1 Kings 19:1–4). And the apostle John, when he was banished to the island of Patmos (Rev. 1:9), faced a test of loneliness. In each case, the trial was brought on by a particular set of circumstances, not by sin.

Temptation

As we reach verse 13 of James 1, there's a shift in focus, from trials to temptation. Webster defines *tempt* as "to entice to do wrong by promise of pleasure or gain."[1] Where the end of trials is growth, the end of temptation is death.

Principles That Apply to Temptation

In verses 13–15, James gives us some principles to remember when temptation comes our way.

Temptation is inevitable.

Let no one say *when* he is tempted . . . (v. 13a, emphasis added)

Notice that the verse doesn't say "if" we are tempted, but "when." The moment we entered this world, we were drafted into a lifelong battle with temptation. The monk living behind the monastery wall struggles with it just like the person who works in a busy downtown office. As Christian soldiers, we are not blamed for having to ward off temptations; none of us can eradicate the presence of these enticements. But we *are* responsible for our reactions to them.

Temptation is never directed by God.

Let no one say when he is tempted, "I am being tempted by God"; for God cannot be tempted by evil, and He Himself does not tempt anyone. (v. 13)

A classic example of what James is referring to has been recorded in Genesis 3:12, where the Lord has just confronted Adam and Eve about disobeying Him. When questioned, Adam immediately responds, "The woman . . . ," trying to shift the focus off himself and

---

1. *Webster's Ninth New Collegiate Dictionary*, see "tempt."

onto Eve. With his next few words, he tries to subtly lay the blame at God's feet: ". . . whom Thou gavest to be with me." Indirectly, Adam is accusing God of setting him up! "Here I was enjoying the bounty and blessing of the Garden of Eden and along came this female that *You* brought into my life. And if it hadn't been for her, I wouldn't have been tempted!"

Is God responsible for temptation in our lives? In James 1:13 the writer points out that God is not even indirectly involved in causing us to sin. When we sin, it is our own choice. Because God's character is holy, pure, totally separate from sin, He cannot be involved in sin. God certainly allows temptation to enter our lives, but we are solely responsible for yielding to it.

Temptation is an individual matter.

> But each one is tempted when he is carried away and enticed by his own lust. (v. 14)

Like metal to a magnet, the sinfulness of our hearts is drawn to temptation. But nothing outside of ourselves, no set of circumstances nor any allurement, is strong enough in itself to force us to sin. Sin occurs when we agree to the temptation and get involved with it.

Temptation that leads to sin always follows the same process.

There are four steps to giving in to temptation, as we see in verses 14–15.

> But each one is tempted when he is carried away and enticed by his own lust. Then when lust has conceived, it gives birth to sin; and when sin is accomplished, it brings forth death.

First: *The bait is dropped.* We can be hooked by a temptation like a fish by a worm because we're hungry . . . hungry for the fulfillment of our physical and spiritual needs. God promises to provide for these needs, but Satan also knows about our hungers. And although he cannot force us to eat, he is a skilled angler at knowing when, where, and how to drop bait in our paths for luring us away from God.

Second: *Our inner desire is attracted to the bait.* The Greek word used for *enticed* is a fishing term. We all know that a hook baited with light bulbs won't catch many fish! In order to pull that fish out from its comfortable hiding place, we've got to find a bait that will interest it, one that it can't resist. Once that bait is dropped and the fish sees it, it's as good as caught.

However, the more we seek God's kingdom and righteousness, and the more we draw from Him our strength and our delight—the less we will be interested in the tempting bait that is continually dropped around us. The point is not that the Lord will remove all temptation; it is that the closer we draw to Him, the less temptation will appeal to us.

Third: *Sin occurs when we yield to temptation.* When we allow temptation to join the sinful desires within the womb of our minds, it gives birth to sin.

Fourth: *Sin results in tragic consequences.* Even though sin sometimes brings a temporary period of pleasure, it always spawns consequences. Satan tries to blur our vision to these consequences by intoxicating us with the wine of pleasure or gain. But that pleasure has a high cost of hurt to ourselves, to others, and to the Lord.

Practical Suggestions for Overcoming Temptation

Now that we have an understanding of temptation, we need to complete our basic training by applying the following five principles —some practical weapons we can use in our day-to-day struggle to resist temptation.

I must counteract temptation, not tolerate it.

James warns us that we are to actively resist sin, not passively tolerate it. For instance, if certain kinds of music, magazines, or films bring before you alluring images, then by allowing them in your life you're not counteracting sin and temptation, you're tolerating it. How often do we pray for deliverance from some temptation only to turn right around and expose ourselves to it? As someone has said, "To pray against temptations, and yet to rush into occasions, is to thrust your fingers into the fire, and then pray they might not be burnt."[2]

I must use the right resistance.

The technique of resistance must match the particular temptation—not all temptations can be handled the same way. For example, every time sensual sins are mentioned in the New Testament, we are told to flee, to run, to get away. That's exactly what Joseph did when his master's wife tried to seduce him (Gen. 39:1–12). For the one who wrestles with the temptation to get rich, the Scriptures teach that you can subdue it by being generous (see 1 Tim. 6:9–10,

2. Thomas Secker, *The New Dictionary of Thoughts* (Standard Book Co., 1960), p. 663.

17–19). If your living or working environment is laden with temptations, Proverbs 4:25 gives the practical suggestion of putting the leash of self-control on your wandering eyes to keep them looking straight ahead. Although our tactics may vary as we go through the different seasons of our lives, we must never be lulled into feeling we have arrived at some spiritual plateau and are no longer vulnerable.

I must remind myself that the final pain will erase the temporary pleasure.

Remember how you used to love to dip your finger into the chocolate icing before it went on the cake? And how that rich, sugary concoction convinced you that you were going to die if you didn't eat the whole bowl? And how after you had sneaked out on the back porch and eaten the whole thing, you wished you *could* die? We can all identify with suffering the consequences of our actions, whether it's from eating a bowl of icing or doing something much more serious. We must cultivate in ourselves the same faith that guarded Moses:

> By faith Moses, when he had grown up, refused to be
> called the son of Pharaoh's daughter; choosing rather
> to endure ill-treatment with the people of God, than
> to enjoy the passing pleasures of sin. (Heb. 11:24–25)

I must control my thought life through Scripture memorization.

Listed among the fruits of the Spirit in Galatians 5:22–23 is the term *self-control.* Its Greek definition suggests "mastering one's drive and the impulses of the will." One way to gain self-control is by memorizing Scripture, as Psalm 119 suggests.[3]

> How can a young man keep his way pure?
> By keeping it according to Thy word. . . .
> Thy word I have treasured in my heart,
> That I may not sin against Thee.
> (vv. 9, 11)

Scripture memorization not only can help us focus on the right things, but it can also come to our aid in resisting a persuasive

---

3. Some have reasoned that since self-control is a fruit of the Spirit, then it is the Spirit who does the active resisting. We're just to play a passive role—simply "let go and let God." Self-control does come from God, but it is up to us to pave the way for it through active involvement of our wills, not through passive observation from the backseat. If we are irresolute with temptation, it will break down our halfhearted walls and conquer us every time.

enticement. Each time Satan tried to tempt Jesus in the wilderness, Jesus used Scripture—God's wisdom—to rebuke the tempter (Matt. 4:1–11).

I must do battle on a daily basis.

This principle is one of consistency. Just because you successfully resist a particular temptation once doesn't mean you have conquered it forever. Temptation often comes whispering, and over time it gradually erodes our will to resist. C. S. Lewis, in his book *The Screwtape Letters*, cleverly exposes this subtlety through a fictitious letter written by an older devil, Screwtape, to his young nephew, Wormwood.

> My Dear Wormwood,
> Obviously you are making excellent progress. My only fear is lest in attempting to hurry the patient you awaken him to a sense of his real position. For you and I, who see that position as it really is, must never forget how totally different it ought to appear to him. We know that we have introduced a change of direction in his course which is already carrying him out of his orbit around the Enemy [God]; but he must be made to imagine that all the choices which have effected this change of course are trivial and revocable. He must not be allowed to suspect that he is now, however slowly, heading right away from the sun on a line which will carry him into the cold and dark of utmost space.[4]

A Final Thought

Mark Antony's most widely known and costly temptation floated to him on a barge. Bedecked as dazzling bait, Cleopatra sailed up the Cydnus River straight into Mark Antony's unguarded heart. Their adulterous relationship with its "passing pleasures" cost him his wife, his place as a world leader, and ultimately his life. Manipulated by Cleopatra into believing she was dead, this "colossal child" fell on his sword, committing suicide out of devotion to what was once only a temptation, something that could have been avoided.

What temptation is drifting alluringly into your life right now? As your mouth waters and your hands reach, have you considered the cost of giving in?

---

4. C. S. Lewis, *The Screwtape Letters* (Chicago, Ill.: Lord and King Associates, distributed by Fleming H. Revell Co., 1976), p. 65.

Living Insights

Temptation is inevitable. That's sobering news—but it should motivate us to become better prepared to face temptation's attacks. One way to prepare ourselves would be to take a closer look at James 1:13–15. If we examine the verbs used in this passage, we can round out our understanding of its meaning.

- Spend a few minutes checking out a concordance, dictionary, or Bible dictionary to see why James might have chosen these particular verbs. For added insight, you might also want to look up other verses where these verbs are used.

James 1:13–15

"Tempted" (vv. 13–14): _____

_____

_____

"Carried away" (v. 14): _____

_____

_____

"Enticed" (v. 14): _____

_____

_____

"Conceived" (v. 15): _____

_____

_____

"Gives birth" (v. 15): _____

_____

_____

"Accomplished" (v. 15): _____

_____

_____

"Brings forth" (v. 15): _____

_____

_____

How much serious thought have you given to counteracting temptation in your life? Use the following exercise to help you home in on this problem.

- Are you on your own when it comes to temptation, or are you accountable to someone for your actions? Think of someone you could ask to help you stick to your goals of overcoming certain temptations, and jot down that person's name.

  _____

- What areas pose the greatest threat to you? Are you most vulnerable to sensual temptations? Or to materialism? How about gossip? Write down the area you would most like to gain control of.

  _____

- Think through some specific ways to overcome temptation in that main area of struggle. Discuss your ideas with your friend, making sure your plan is realistic, attainable, and simple.

  _____

  _____

  _____

  _____

  _____

Chapter 5

THE PROBLEM OF DEPRESSION

Selected Scripture

In the fall of 1900, the Texas gulf coast city of Galveston lost more than six thousand of its citizens. They died at the hands of a violent hurricane that bludgeoned the unsuspecting people with its winds and accompanying tidal waves.

Today, another storm rages with a different kind of devastation. It's one we don't hear about on the evening news, yet it darkens the skies and pounds the inner shores of people all across the world. Even those pristine islands of hope traditionally inhabited by our children are being ravaged by it in unprecedented numbers.

That storm is called depression. Its enervating winds beat us down and its encroaching flood waters deluge us with despair. The National Institute of Health estimates that each year in the United States approximately seventy-five thousand desperate people succumb to depression's undertow through acts of suicide.[1] Their faces disappear from the surface of a sea of other human faces struggling to survive this storm's unrelenting blast.

In the physical world, satellites monitor atmospheric conditions and give us warnings against threatening storms. But storm warnings and watches for tempests of the soul are best provided by people who have faced similar emotional storms.

Three men in the Bible—Moses, Elijah, and Jonah—each had depression hit him full force. Their joy was eclipsed by oppressive clouds of worthlessness, guilt, and apprehension. They heard the winds of despair and discouragement wail through their hearts. And they almost drowned in the flood waters of hopelessness.

To gain a helpful understanding of this devastating storm, let's examine the physical, emotional, and spiritual conditions that precipitated the depression of these men.

---

1. Paul R. Welter, *Counseling and the Search for Meaning,* Resources for Christian Counseling (Waco, Tex.: Word Books, 1987), vol. 9, p. 25.

Moses

Despite the fact that they had been privileged with God's miraculous leading, the children of Israel had done nothing but complain since they left Egypt. God had miraculously opened Pharaoh's hand and the Red Sea so they could enter a new future, but they complained that that future was impossible. God miraculously gave them manna to eat, but they griped about the menu. God miraculously gave them water, but they grumbled about its taste.

The trip to the Promised Land that had begun as an adventure with God had deteriorated into a nightmare for Moses. Nothing seemed to satisfy the two million whiny Israelites in the backseat of this trip. Day in, day out, their complaints and criticisms assaulted Moses' ears until, finally, he was ready to pull over and call it quits.

> Now Moses heard the people weeping throughout their families, each man at the doorway of his tent; and the anger of the Lord was kindled greatly, and Moses was displeased. (Num. 11:10)

The last phrase literally means "and Moses was *depressed.*" Like an exasperated parent, Moses exploded, pouring out his pent-up frustrations and utter despair to the Lord.

> "Why hast Thou been so hard on Thy servant? And why have I not found favor in Thy sight, that Thou hast laid the burden of all this people on me? Was it I who conceived all this people? Was it I who brought them forth, that Thou shouldest say to me, 'Carry them in your bosom as a nurse carries a nursing infant, to the land which Thou didst swear to their fathers'? Where am I to get meat to give to all this people? For they weep before me, saying, 'Give us meat that we may eat!' I alone am not able to carry all this people, because it is too burdensome for me." (vv. 11–14)

In his words we can hear the rumblings of depression's storm: "Enough is enough! I can't take it anymore! I'm finished, I quit, I resign." Then Moses rang out a final thunderclap, "Kill me . . . do not let me see my wretchedness" (v. 15).

Why did Moses feel so dejected and ready to die? How could someone who had spoken with God and seen His miraculous power ever be so depressed? Let's track the buildup of his depression through three areas.

Physically

Moses had a leadership problem. He had tried to do all the work himself, and, as a result, he had stretched himself so thin that he snapped like a taut rubber band.[2] He was simply exhausted, with no reserves of physical strength left to ward off the onslaught of depression.

Emotionally

Moses was also suffering from feelings of inferiority—he didn't feel equal to his task (v. 14). He had tried to shoulder the weight of all the people's burdens, and it had only succeeded in crushing the emotional life out of him. He had taken all their problems on himself, instead of letting them take responsibility for their own lives.

Spiritually

Moses felt distant from God and was beginning to wonder, "Lord, what have You got against me?" (v. 11). He had become consumed by his work rather than his God—and God's recommendation for rejuvenation was simple: "Back off! Slow down! Delegate the work. You're doing enough for seventy people!" (vv. 16–17). Through this simple plan Moses would rekindle the embers of his relationship with God and regain the perspective that the Lord alone was responsible for the people's growth.

Elijah

The climate preceding Elijah's depression had been "mostly sunny and dry" . . . literally. For the past three years, the sun had blistered the land and its people through the clear skies of a prophesied drought. Basking in this arid atmosphere was a cultic group called Baal's prophets, until Elijah came and cleared out this den of vipers, who had been injecting the people with the poison of idol worship.

When the maleficent Queen Jezebel heard that Elijah had killed the brood of prophets that she had engendered, she reacted with a flash flood of fury that was poured into a message for Elijah.

---

2. We know this is the case from verse 16, where the Lord instructs Moses to gather seventy other men to share the burden of leading the people. Back in Exodus 18, we see that Moses has been warned once before about this tendency to take too much on himself. However, it appears that Moses had failed to apply those principles in his current situation.

"So may the gods do to me and even more, if I do not make your life as the life of one of them by tomorrow about this time." (1 Kings 19:2b)

Elijah the prophet quickly became Elijah the fugitive, trying to outrun the oncoming storm.

And he was afraid and arose and ran for his life and came to Beersheba, which belongs to Judah, and left his servant there. But he himself went a day's journey into the wilderness, and came and sat down under a juniper tree; and he requested for himself that he might die, and said, "It is enough; now, O Lord, take my life, for I am not better than my fathers." (vv. 3–4)

He had gone from exulting on a mountaintop to crouching under a juniper tree, which may as well have been a weeping willow. "Lord, I quit! Take my life!" Sound familiar? Let's look at the causes.

Physically

Like Moses, Elijah was totally exhausted. He had just been through three years of famine; faced and slain 450 prophets of Baal alone in an intense, daylong confrontation; missed several meals and lots of sleep; been in intense prayer; been up and down Mount Carmel twice; made a thirty-mile run down to Jezreel, outracing Ahab's chariot; received a death threat; fled for his life to Beersheba; and traveled another day's journey into the wilderness.

Emotionally

Elijah was suffering from a martyr complex. His feelings of self-pity reflect that his focus was on himself.

"I have been very zealous for the Lord, the God of hosts; for the sons of Israel have forsaken Thy covenant, torn down Thine altars and killed Thy prophets with the sword. And I alone am left; and they seek my life, to take it away." (v. 10)

"I'm all alone. There's nobody else. I'm the only one standing true to the cause!" Elijah couldn't see past the fog of his own self-absorption.

Spiritually

Elijah's spiritual condition can be diagnosed from his response to Jezebel's death threat, "And he was afraid" (v. 3). Up to that moment, through the recent flurry of events, Elijah had kept his eyes on the Lord. Now they were on his enemy, and his knees were knocking.

God began this worn-out prophet's rehabilitation by sending him food. As with Moses, He gave no rebuke for experiencing depression . . . no long, preachy sermons with seventeen points. He simply said, "You need a good meal, Elijah; eat" (vv. 5–7).

Then God began to revitalize Elijah's emotional and spiritual strength through step-by-step doses. First, He revealed Himself, helping Elijah get his focus back where it belonged (vv. 11–13). Next, He corrected Elijah's perspective by reminding him he wasn't alone—there were seven thousand others who also had not bowed down to Baal (v. 18). And finally, the Lord gave him a friend who would minister to him (vv. 19–21).

Jonah

Strangely enough, the event that led to Jonah's depression was the repentance of the entire city of Nineveh. Fresh from the greatest revival recorded in God's Word, Jonah's response was far from ecstatic.

It greatly displeased Jonah, and he became angry. (Jon. 4:1)

To understand this confusing reaction, let's look again at the contributing factors.

Physically

Only a few days earlier, Jonah had been sleeping aboard a ship bound for Tarshish; now he was standing exhausted at the gates of Nineveh. His unusual itinerary had included being thrown overboard into a stormy sea, spending three days in the stomach of a great fish, and then being regurgitated onto dry land in a smelly inauguration of his preaching career at Nineveh. Once there, he had to traverse the heathen city and cry out the message of repentance to a people he didn't know and didn't like.[3] He was beat.

---

3. There are at least two reasons for Jonah's hostile attitude toward Nineveh. First, the city was the capital of Assyria, "one of the cruelest, vilest, most powerful, and most idolatrous empires in the world" (*The Bible Knowledge Commentary*, ed. John F. Walvoord and Roy B. Zuck [New York, N.Y.: Scripture Press Publications, Victor Books, 1985], p. 1494). And second, as Martin Luther wrote in his *Commentary on the Prophet Jonah*, "Because Jonah was sorry that God was so kind, he would rather not preach, yea, would rather die, than that the grace of God, which was to be the peculiar privilege of the people of Israel, should be communicated to the Gentiles

Emotionally

Jonah began stirring up the winds of his own depression because he was furious with God for not bringing judgment on a people he despised.

> And he prayed to the Lord and said, "Please Lord, was not this what I said while I was still in my own country? Therefore, in order to forestall this I fled to Tarshish, for I knew that Thou art a gracious and compassionate God, slow to anger and abundant in lovingkindness, and one who relents concerning calamity. Therefore now, O Lord, please take my life from me, for death is better to me than life." (vv. 2–3)

The bitterness in his soul was being nurtured by a superiority complex, an arrogant bigotry molded by ethnic pride.

Spiritually

Jonah didn't want the Ninevites to repent and be spared God's wrathful judgment, so he was angry with God. At this point, his relationship with the Lord was being blocked by resentment.

So God used a question to help break up the egotistical clouds of Jonah's depression.

> And the Lord said, "Do you have good reason to be angry?" (v. 4)

Instead of answering, Jonah built himself a shelter outside Nineveh to "see what would happen in the city" (v. 5), and eventually he begged to die (v. 8). God approached him again with a question similar to the one before; then He cleared the skies of Jonah's overcast heart with truth (vv. 9–11).

Storm Warnings

As we studied the depression of these three men, did any personal wind-warning flags begin to flap in your mind? Did you recognize yourself in Moses—are you overworked, trying to do it all alone, feeling governed by inferiority's cruel barbs, constantly taking on guilt over things you can't control, feeling distant from God, wondering whatever happened to that God of power you believe in?

---

also, who had neither the word of God, nor the laws of Moses, nor the worship of God, nor prophets, nor anything else, but rather strove against God, and His word, and His people" (as quoted by C. F. Keil and F. Delitzsch, in *Commentary on the Old Testament* [reprint, Grand Rapids, Mich.: William B. Eerdmans Publishing Co., 1978], vol. 10, p. 392).

Or are you more like Elijah—caught up in a martyr complex, the eyes of your heart having lost their focus on God, feeling the need for a friend's support, feeling pursued and threatened?

Or did you see yourself in Jonah—superior and smug, downright angry at God, flailing others with the whip of a judgmental attitude?

Is exhaustion the only one who greets you at the door when you arrive home from work every day? Do you feel confused because a happy event has left you depressed instead of grateful and at peace? Are you at the end of your rope, like all three of these men, entertaining thoughts about death?

Whether your current forecast is for clear skies or severe weather, here are five important points that will provide you with cover from the full force of depression's storm.

Realize that depression is not a sin but a symptom.

Depression is like the flashing warning light on the dashboard of a car. The way to extinguish it is not by smashing the light, but by lifting the hood and finding the problem. When depression sets in, something deeper is probably wrong. We need to look into its root causes.

Maintain a consistent program of relaxation.

Leisure is fast becoming a lost art to the people who worship at the altar of careers. And the result of this frantic religion is often depression. People who have mastered the art of building leisure into their lives usually experience fewer problems with depression.

Guard against those subtle complexes.

To keep from falling into inferiority, superiority, or martyr complexes, we need to keep our eyes focused on Christ. And we also need to develop deep friendships, so people will be there to lift us out of the complexes if we do fall.

Remember God is for you, not against you.

One of the greatest verses in all the New Testament is found in Romans 8: "If God is for us, who is against us?" (v. 31). It is not God's design to make our lives miserable, but meaningful.

Never forget that Satan can bring depression.

Depression is one of the sharpest darts of the enemy. But here's the good news: "Greater is He who is in you than he who is in the world" (1 John 4:4b).

Have you been struggling with depression lately? It's difficult, isn't it? But it's encouraging to remember that you aren't alone— even God's chosen leaders in the Bible got depressed, and just as God helped them, He can help you too.

* Let's carefully study how God helped Moses, Elijah, and Jonah with their depression. Reread the following passages, and write down what you notice about God's response to their problems. Was He gentle? Was He angry? Did He give them long, scolding lectures? Was He patient? What can you learn about God's character from these situations?

Numbers 11:10–17 _____

_____

_____

_____

_____

_____

1 Kings 19:1–21 _____

_____

_____

_____

_____

Jonah 4:1–11 _____

_____

_____

_____

_____

In looking at the causes of depression, we followed a definite pattern—we looked at physical, emotional, and spiritual conditions in each of the men we studied. Examining our own situations with this same pattern will help us identify our feelings and hopefully detect any signs of oncoming trouble.

• Write down how you're doing in each of the following areas. If you're not on top of the world, that's OK. You don't need to worry about measuring up to anyone else's expectations or demands here. Feel free to tell it like it really is.

Physically

_____

_____

_____

_____

Emotionally

_____

_____

_____

_____

Spiritually

_____

_____

_____

_____

• Conclude this time in prayer, asking God what His therapy might be for you.

Chapter 6

THE PROBLEM OF WORRY
Matthew 6:25–34

The soul lies hidden within like a subterranean cave, but with the light of divine assistance, King Solomon was able to probe its deepest recesses. One of the things he saw is recorded in Proverbs 14:13a: "Even in laughter the heart may be in pain."

What Solomon means is that things are not always as they appear. The light of smiles and laughter may warm the surface of our lives, while the darkness of pain chills the inner depths of our hearts.

Seeping down into the deep interior caverns of our souls is worry. Its metronomic dripping forms piercing stalactites of anxiety, drip by drip, layer upon layer. And although laughter may echo in these hidden chambers, it is a laughter barnacled with worry.

Today, let's examine worry with a view to stopping its flow into our hearts and dissolving its crusty shroud within.

Biblical Perspective

If you were to search through a concordance, it might surprise you to find that *worry* is not listed. The Bible actually says much about worry, but the word itself goes by several different aliases, such as *care, anxiety, burden, trouble,* and *fear.*

In fact, in Matthew 6:25–34, Jesus uses the word *anxious* no less than five times. A background check reveals that its origins are tied to the meaning "to be divided or distracted." So the mission of *worry,* this invisible insurgent, is always to trouble or distress us. It incites a mental and emotional riot that works against our ability to focus on what we're doing.

Specific Arguments against Worry

In verse 24 Jesus makes it clear that we must choose between two masters—either God or materialism. If we choose to serve God, worry will inevitably try to distract us from that service. Let's take a careful look at the rest of chapter 6, where we'll be able to draw out five arguments against worry from what Jesus has to say.

First: *Worry keeps you from enjoying what you have.*

> "For this reason I say to you, do not be anxious for your
> life, as to what you shall eat, or what you shall drink;
> nor for your body, as to what you shall put on. Is not life
> more than food, and the body than clothing?" (v. 25)

We live in a society whose basic philosophic foodstuffs gorge our
worries and only tease our hungry souls. This mind-set tries to con-
vince us that life is only about food and designer clothing labels.
And those who are willing to swallow this philosophy develop robust
anxieties—anxieties that rob them of the ability to enjoy what they
have by keeping their eyes on the things they don't have.[1]

Second: *Worry makes you forget your worth.*

> "Look at the birds of the air, that they do not sow,
> neither do they reap, nor gather into barns, and yet
> your heavenly Father feeds them. Are you not worth
> much more than they?" (v. 26)

There are well over eight thousand species of birds, and God
feeds them all—even those baby rose-breasted grosbeaks that eat
426 times in eleven hours![2] Yet for all their beauty and diversity,
Jesus did not die for a single bird. He died for us. It's hard to believe we could ever doubt our value in God's sight, yet when worry
pours its acid through our minds, it blanches our memory of the
Savior's love.

Third: *Worry is completely useless.*

> "And which of you by being anxious can add a single
> cubit to his life's span?" (v. 27)

We can lie awake and fret all we want, but when morning comes,
we'll still have problems. So why do we do it? Because somewhere
deep within us is a secret love of worrying. We enjoy entertaining
worries. There is always a line of new ones waiting to get in the
door—as we shove one out the back door, we usher a new one in
the front. When one worry is gone, we immediately replace it with
another.

Fourth: *Worry erases the promises of God from your mind.*

---

1. Does Jesus mean that people should not provide for their households? No. To
neglect this responsibility is to be "worse than an unbeliever" (1 Tim. 5:8). The
balance is to be diligent at our work, but not assume responsibilities God never
intended us to handle—that's worry.

2. *Compton's Pictured Encyclopedia* (Chicago, Ill.: F. E. Compton and Co., 1932),
vol. 2, p. 122.

"But if God so arrays the grass of the field, which is alive today and tomorrow is thrown into the furnace, will He not much more do so for you, O men of little faith? Do not be anxious then, saying, 'What shall we eat?' or 'What shall we drink?' or 'With what shall we clothe ourselves?'" (vv. 30–31)

When times are lean, it's easy to forget how much God cares about us. Our natural tendency is to check in at worry's twenty-four-hour-a-day clinic instead of asking the Great Physician to make a house call on our lives. Memories of God's promises slip from our consciousness as worry administers massive doses of self-absorption, until we are like spiritual amnesiacs who remember only the most basic questions in life: "What will I eat? What will I drink? What will I wear?" We forget that God provides for us, and that He has promised to take care of all our needs (see Rom. 8:31–32).

Fifth: *Worry is characteristic of unbelievers, not Christians.*

"For all these things the Gentiles eagerly seek; for your heavenly Father knows that you need all these things." (Matt. 6:32)

Each day non-Christians face a gauntlet of worries. And the sad part of it is that they must do it alone. As long as they have no heavenly Father to serve, their lives will be spent in servitude to the tyrannical urgings of worry. The Christian, however, can reach out beyond worry's iron hand and find Another's, whose scars reassure us that He is there and He cares for us (Heb. 13:5–6).

These five arguments against worry are essential to know, but, as the saying goes, a picture is worth a thousand words. Tucked away in the book of Genesis are several candid snapshots of worry at work in the family of Abraham. Let's leaf through this family album to cement in our minds the devastating and far-reaching effects worry can have.

A Family of Worriers

Every family is different. From the music of some families, great composers are formed. From the generosity of others, great humanitarians are unselfishly shared. And from the disquieted womb of others, great worriers come trembling forth.

One such family was Abraham's. Although God had promised to make him a great nation (12:1–3), when a famine came, Abraham moved to Egypt and forgot all about God's promise, with worry's distracting help (v. 10). Left to his own resources, he came up with a deceitful plan to protect himself against the imaginary enemies of his fearful mind.

> And it came about when he came near to Egypt, that he said to Sarai his wife, "See now, I know that you are a beautiful woman; and it will come about when the Egyptians see you, that they will say, 'This is his wife'; and they will kill me, but they will let you live. Please say that you are my sister so that it may go well with me because of you, and that I may live on account of you." (vv. 11–13)

You can practically hear the quiver of worry in his words and see his dry lips dehydrated by fear. Trusting in his own plans, Abraham entered Egypt.

> And it came about when Abram came into Egypt, the Egyptians saw that the woman was very beautiful. And Pharaoh's officials saw her and praised her to Pharaoh; and the woman was taken into Pharaoh's house. Therefore he treated Abram well for her sake. (vv. 14–16a)

For a time his scheme worked, and Abraham might have thought that worry really pays off. However, God exposed Abraham's lie (vv. 17–19), and instead of having a great testimony before the pharaoh of Egypt, Abraham ended up being shamefully escorted out of town—all because of worry.

But did Abraham learn his lesson? The answer is in Genesis 20:1–2.

> Now Abraham journeyed from there toward the land of the Negev, and settled between Kadesh and Shur; then he sojourned in Gerar. And Abraham said of Sarah his wife, "She is my sister." So Abimelech king of Gerar sent and took Sarah.

Same song, second verse. Abraham still believed that the "she's my sister" routine was safer than trusting in God's promises. And again the Lord exposed his scheme (vv. 3–7).

But the infamous statement, "She's my sister," didn't stop here. It got passed on to Abraham's son Isaac, like a family heirloom.

In Genesis 26 Isaac faced a set of circumstances that were almost identical to those his father faced in Genesis 12. When the men where Isaac lived asked about his wife, what did the son of Abraham say? "She is my sister" (26:7). And he, too, was caught in his worry-induced deceit and rebuked publicly (vv. 8–11).

All parents bequeath to their children different kinds of legacies. One of Abraham's legacies to his son was the art of worrying. What legacy will you leave to your children?

Practical Applications

After seeing great saints like Abraham and Isaac fail to conquer worry, we poor garden-variety Christians could easily give up hope. But worry isn't something we're stuck with. Jesus ends the passage in Matthew 6 with two practical suggestions: Keep your mind on the Lord, and take one day at a time.

> "But seek first His kingdom and His righteousness; and all these things shall be added to you. Therefore do not be anxious for tomorrow; for tomorrow will care for itself. Each day has enough trouble of its own." (vv. 33–34)

From other passages of Scripture, we can find four more principles to help us break worry's gravitational pull. The first is *presence*—claim the presence of God in your life (see Isa. 41:10). The second is *promises*—get into the Word of God and learn His assurances (see Ps. 119:14–16). Third, *prayer*—pray for specific needs, not just generalities (see Phil. 4:6–7). And last, *patience*—don't allow worry to sell you short and steal the victory that should be yours (see Ps. 27:14).

Worry is like any other sin. It must first come to us as a temptation, begging for a place to stay. That is the critical moment for us all. Will you keep your mind in fellowship with the Lord? Or will you let worry onto the front porch, give it a drink of water, and chat a bit before you send it on its way? You can bet that before you pour its second glass of water, worry will have you asking it to stay for dinner. When worry comes panhandling at your screen door, send Christ to answer its call instead.

Continued on next page

Ulcers, nail-biting, gray hairs, headaches . . . worry can do nothing but produce ill effects in our lives.

- Worry is the subject of Matthew 6:25–34. This passage can give you a whole new perspective on the problems that plague you. As you read it, try to pick out a key word or phrase for each verse. Then conclude by writing a summary statement for the entire passage.

Text	Key Word or Phrase
v. 25	
v. 26	
v. 27	
v. 28	
v. 29	
v. 30	
v. 31	
v. 32	
v. 33	
v. 34	

Summary statement: _____

_____

_____

Take a moment to read Luke 10:38–42, paying particular attention to the cameo performance of Martha. With this scene fresh in
your mind, answer the following questions.

• What was the source of Martha's worry?

_____

_____

• What does Martha imply both of Mary and of Jesus when she
storms out of the kitchen and confronts Jesus?

_____

_____

• With what attitude does Jesus respond to the worrier?

_____

_____

• How is Mary's example a remedy to the problem of worry?

_____

_____

• Which woman most accurately depicts your life?

_____

_____

Chapter 7

THE PROBLEM OF ANGER

Ephesians 4:26–27

Anger—it's an emotional boogeyman in the Christian community. Just the mention of it sends chills down the backbones of many individuals, families, and churches. It has been looked upon as a terrifying emotional monster . . . a violent and uncontrollable Frankenstein. For years, anger has been banished from the society of our acceptable feelings, yet we haven't rid ourselves of it completely. We can still feel it prowling around the edges of our minds, hungry for something to feed on.

No doubt, it would be easy to whip up a lynch mob mentality and go after anger with our hanging ropes. But before we string up all forms of this emotion as vile and despicable, we should step back, calm down, and examine the truth about anger.

Our first step in separating myth from reality is to define anger. Webster says that *anger* is "a strong feeling of displeasure and usu. of antagonism."[1] With this very general definition in mind, let's look at the specific kinds of anger that we encounter where we live.

Various Phases of Anger

Psychologists have noted that anger has at least five phases. First, there is *mild irritation*—a feeling of minor discomfort brought on by someone or something. Next comes *indignation*—frustration over something unfair or unreasonable. From there, indignation transitions into *wrath*—a strong desire to avenge or punish, which never goes unexpressed. Wrath then leads to *fury*—a state that suggests violence and temporary loss of control. Moving into the last phase, the full moon of anger is *rage*—the most dangerous form, where acts of violence are committed by people scarcely aware of what they're doing. Like the father who, in a fit of jealous rage, brutally murdered five people . . . his sister-in-law, his wife, and his three children.

Perhaps the monsters we have learned to fear and despise lurk in these last three phases. And possibly, these phases are why so many people try to keep this emotion locked in the cellars of their hearts, behind doors of denial.

1. *Webster's Ninth New Collegiate Dictionary,* see "anger."

Denying reality, however, is never God's way. Let's examine the Scriptures to learn how God views this powerful feeling.

Observations Concerning Anger

Too often, to be considered "good Christians," we've had to put our anger in cement and drop it to the bottom of our being. Over time, however, this repressed anger ulcerates into bitterness, revenge, and other harmful feelings that leak out and poison the mental, emotional, physical, and spiritual streams which flow from our hearts.

Rather than agreeing with the tradition that commands us to deny our anger, Ephesians 4:26–27 actually encourages us to have it!

Be angry, and yet do not sin; do not let the sun go down on your anger, and do not give the devil an opportunity.

With the first two words, the apostle Paul destroys one of the great myths of the Christian faith—that we should never be angry. If nothing remained in verse 26 but the first two words, grammatically you would end them with an exclamation point: "Be angry!" We are commanded by God to "Get mad!" With the rest of that phrase, Paul dispels the myth that all anger is sin. And from this truth, we can make several observations.

Anger is a God-given emotion.

All of us are grateful that God has endowed us with His ability to feel emotions. But why do many of us keep trying to give back the gift of anger? Where did we get the idea that it is more like God to never get angry—to treat anger as an unwanted emotional appendage that good Christians learn to simply cut off? Instead of continually trying to perform an emotional lobotomy on ourselves to be rid of anger, we should thank God for it.

Anger is not necessarily sinful.

Eighteen times in the Old Testament alone, the anger of the Lord is recorded. Eighteen times God felt angry over sin, and not one of those times was He being sinful. In the New Testament, Jesus plaited a whip of thongs and drove out the moneychangers with that same feeling of anger (John 2:13–16). And now God is saying to His sons and daughters in Christ to do the same: "Be angry, and yet do not sin." It's as though someone were to say to you, "Now when you go out tonight, enjoy yourself. Have a good time—but not at the expense of others." It could also be compared to what the apostle says in 1 John: "I want you to love, but don't love the things of the world" (see 2:15). In the same way, we are being told, "Be angry, but don't carry that anger to the point of its becoming sin."

Anger must have safeguards.

All hot water heaters have an important safeguard built into them called a pop-off valve. When excessive heat and steam build up too much pressure inside, the pop-off valve automatically blows and releases it. But what about you and me? What do we do when anger is boiling inside of us? Instead of popping off, which only works well for water heaters, Paul gives us two practical safeguards for keeping anger from exploding into sin.

First: *"Do not let the sun go down on your anger"* (Eph. 4:26). In Paul's day, before electric lights, the setting of the sun marked the closing of the day. All accounts of anger still open at that time were to be cleared out so there would be no anger on the books going into the night. Even with electric lights, this is still an excellent principle. Because it is when we prolong our anger that we give sin an opportunity to come in.

Second: *"Do not give the devil an opportunity"* (v. 27). Do not allow your anger to be expressed in such a way that the devil's character is reproduced in you. Uncontrolled anger is a wide open door for Satan. He will enter it every time and set to work replacing his character and his witness for that of Christ's.

Examples of Justifiable Anger

"We're out of toilet paper?" "Who ate all the Cap'n Crunch?" "You threw away the funnies?" Even though all of us have gotten angry over trivial things like these, this type of anger is not always biblically justifiable. Which brings us to the question, What type of anger *is* justifiable? When can we say that it is right to be angry?

When God's Word and Will Are Consciously Disobeyed

After forty days and nights on a mountain capped by the glory of God, it was time for Moses to rejoin his people. In his hands were the heavy stone tablets on which God had written the Ten Commandments. However, on the way down, Moses' mind was invaded by the troubling scene of a people who had promised to do all the Lord had told them—but didn't.

> And it came about, as soon as Moses came near the camp, that he saw the calf and the dancing; and Moses' anger burned, and he threw the tablets from his hands

and shattered them at the foot of the mountain. And he took the calf which they had made and burned it with fire, and ground it to powder, and scattered it over the surface of the water, and made the sons of Israel drink it. (Exod. 32:19–20)

The profane and open rebellion of the Israelites ignited a burning anger that roared in the furnace of Moses' heart. It is this same kind of justified anger that should crackle in the heart of every Christian who sees the will of God openly disobeyed by other believers.

When Enemies Move into Realms outside Their Rights and Jurisdiction

An example of enemies overstepping their bounds is recorded in 1 Samuel 11, where Nahash the Ammonite declared war on the people of Israel in Jabesh-gilead. Messengers brought the threatening news to the people of Gibeah, whose weeping caught the attention of Saul, their anointed king.

Now behold, Saul was coming from the field behind the oxen; and he said, "What is the matter with the people that they weep?" So they related to him the words of the men of Jabesh.
Then the Spirit of God came upon Saul mightily when he heard these words, and he became very angry. (vv. 5–6)

Saul burned with the same anger that ignited the embers of Isaiah's warning, "Woe to those who . . . take away the rights of the ones who are in the right!" (Isa. 5:22–23).

When Parents Are Unfair with Children

In our final example of justifiable anger, let's rejoin Paul in Ephesians, where he deals with the sensitive issue of the parent-child relationship in the home.

And, fathers, do not provoke your children to anger; but bring them up in the discipline and instruction of the Lord. (6:4)

Here, as well as in Colossians 3:21, the parent specifically addressed is the father. The Lord seems to be in tune with the fact that fathers in particular have a tendency to exasperate their children. Especially dads who are given to impatience and don't take time to understand feelings. Especially those fathers who get into their steamrollers and flatten important family discussions with quick-fix answers and demands that are unfair. When obedient

53

children are dealt with unfairly time and time again, they will respond in anger, and this anger is justified. Now this is not a carte blanche statement for children to feel that they are being provoked by everything their father says. It is a warning to fathers especially, to deal with their children fairly and with understanding.

A Final Thought

A study such as this can evoke a lot of feelings. Many of you may feel relieved to know, for the first time, that it's OK to be angry. For others, you may be surprised that there's a type of anger which doesn't backhand you or lock you out with a raging silence or cruelly drag your most vulnerable intimacies out to public ridicule.

Anger has its place alongside compassion and love in our God-given emotional repertoire. We have all suffered from its abuses, just as we have from some of our other emotions, but that doesn't negate its positive role. So instead of attempting to deny it, let's allow God to teach us how to control this valuable asset.

 Living Insights

Let's dig deeper into the Scriptures to explore the whole subject of anger. In the list that follows are eight references relating to anger. Look up each one and summarize what it says.

Scripture	Summary Statement
Gen. 4:3–7	_____
	_____
Ps. 30:5	_____
	_____
Ps. 103:8–9	_____
	_____
Prov. 14:29	_____
	_____
Prov. 22:24–25	_____
	_____

Prov. 29:22 _____

_____

Matt. 5:21–24 _____

_____

James 1:19–20 _____

_____

🍇 *Living Insights* STUDY TWO

It's possible that this is the first time you've ever really thought of anger as God-given. Maybe you have never considered anger justifiable. Let's take some time to develop that side of our study.

• Can you think of some incidents from your past where anger was justified? List a few.

_____

_____

_____

_____

• How would you resolve the tension between verses like Ephesians 4:26 and James 1:20?

_____

_____

_____

_____

• What types of things generally get you angry?

_____

_____

_____

_____

Chapter 8

A COOL HAND
ON A HOT HEAD

Selected Proverbs

Mark Twain once said, "Everyone is a moon, and has a dark side which he never shows to anybody."[1]

In our last lesson, we looked at the righteous side of anger and learned that we don't need to be afraid of this feeling—sometimes, in fact, it is the appropriate response to make. Today, though, we need to travel to the darker side of this mercurial emotion, exploring the kinds of anger that send us spinning out of control . . . the unjustified types of anger.

Now this doesn't necessarily mean that we're breaking chairs over each other's heads or screaming our lungs out at one another. Unjustified, out of control anger can be much more subtle than this. But the damage it produces in others as well as ourselves is just as real.

Hopefully, after today's study we'll recognize areas where we may be letting anger get out of control and find comfort and direction as we let the cool hand of Solomon's counsel rest on our hot heads of anger.

Illustrations of Unjustifiable Anger

Before we allow the telescope of memory to focus on the meteoric furies of others, let's examine ourselves to find out just how much influence the following three kinds of unjustified anger have had on our lives.

When Anger Comes from the Wrong Motive

There are any number of flinty motives that can ignite the wrong kind of anger. One type is jealousy. In Luke 15 we find a familiar story with a less familiar character, who is the picture of jealous anger. As we enter the scene, a welcome-home party is in progress for a prodigal son who has just returned.

---

1. Mark Twain, in *Bartlett's Familiar Quotations*, 14th ed., rev. and enl., ed. Emily Morison Beck (Boston, Mass.: Little, Brown and Co., 1968), p. 763.

"Now his older son was in the field, and when he came and approached the house, he heard music and dancing. And he summoned one of the servants and began inquiring what these things might be. And he said to him, 'Your brother has come, and your father has killed the fattened calf, because he has received him back safe and sound.' But he became angry, and was not willing to go in; and his father came out and began entreating him. But he answered and said to his father, 'Look! For so many years I have been serving you, and I have never neglected a command of yours; and yet you have never given me a kid, that I might be merry with my friends; but when this son of yours came, who has devoured your wealth with harlots, you killed the fattened calf for him.'" (vv. 25–30)

Not "my brother" but "this son of yours." The older brother's jealous anger had already begun to burn bridges between himself and his younger brother. That same kind of jealousy can cause friction in us as well, such as when another person receives some kind of commendation, promotion, or attention that we feel we deserve. The thing we have to ask ourselves when our anger begins to spark is, Why am I at *this* moment getting angry? What's my motive? Is it jealousy, pride, revenge? With the Holy Spirit's help, we can discover the root of our anger and deal with it before it starts burning out of control.

When Things Don't Go Our Way

It seems that when things don't go our way, what usually comes our way is a testy, unjustified anger—similar to one that visited Jonah.

God had commissioned His reluctant prophet to preach to the city of Nineveh. However, Jonah wanted God to destroy those people instead of offering them any chance of repentance. In the end, the stubborn evangelist did preach God's message and the entire city repented and rejoiced—while Jonah fumed.

When God saw their deeds, that they turned from their wicked way, then God relented concerning the calamity which He had declared He would bring upon them. And He did not do it.
But it greatly displeased Jonah, and he became angry. (Jon. 3:10–4:1)

Jonah didn't get the destruction he had wanted, and he was furious. So he stalked away from God, built himself a shelter, and sat down to pout. But that's not the end of the story.

So the Lord God appointed a plant and it grew up over Jonah to be a shade over his head to deliver him from his discomfort. And Jonah was extremely happy about the plant. But God appointed a worm when dawn came the next day, and it attacked the plant and it withered. And it came about when the sun came up that God appointed a scorching east wind, and the sun beat down on Jonah's head so that he became faint and begged with all his soul to die, saying, "Death is better to me than life."

Then God said to Jonah, "Do you have good reason to be angry about the plant?" And he said, "I have good reason to be angry, even to death." (vv. 6–9)

Can't you just hear his whining? "You made me uncomfortable, and I don't like it when I get hot, and now that I'm hot *and* didn't get my way about Nineveh, I have every reason to be angry!"

Jonah was consumed with the kind of anger we often feel when we get a flat tire, when people on the freeway are not driving to suit us, or when it rains on the day we're going to Disneyland. Underneath our muttering is an attitude of "I've got my rights! I have a right to a perfectly smooth trip. I have a right to a clear lane when I'm in a hurry. I have a right to a sunny day whenever I want to be outdoors!" But where is that written? We can sound pretty ridiculous when we strip away the anger that hides our selfish demands.

But perhaps this ridiculousness can save us from blowing our tops. "A joyful heart is good medicine," Proverbs 17:22a tells us, and laughter can make all the difference in the world. Seeing the humor in a situation is one of the best ways to handle it when we don't get our way. It's our choice; either we learn to laugh at ourselves, or we live on the edge of anger twenty-four hours a day.

When We React Too Quickly

When we fly off the handle without investigating the facts, we are sinning. The counsel of Solomon and of the apostle James, although centuries apart, both illustrate this point.

The end of a matter is better than its beginning;[2]
Patience of spirit is better than haughtiness of spirit.

---

2. The point Solomon is making here is that we should hear the person out—get past the beginning of the story and wait till the end. This is reaffirmed in Proverbs 18:13, "He who gives an answer before he hears, It is folly and shame to him."

Do not be eager in your heart to be angry,
For anger resides in the bosom of fools. (Eccles. 7:8–9)

But let everyone be quick to hear, slow to speak and
slow to anger. (James 1:19b)

Many of us live on the brink of irritation because we are caught
up in the fast pace of this world. Our overcommitted schedules drive
us through the day in a frenzied pace that prompts us to hear only
half of what the other person is saying before we respond. And like
a half-cocked pistol, just a little pressure on the trigger is enough to
set us off.

The best way to disarm this volatile reaction is to cultivate the
art of quietness. It's amazing how much more patient and tolerant
we become when things are quiet around us. And a good way to
start doing this is to turn off the noisemakers in our lives for awhile—
the radio, for instance, and especially the TV. The weaning process
may be difficult, but without the vital practice of solitude and quietness, we will never become mature men and women of God.

Advice on Dealing with Anger

The great American statesman Thomas Jefferson had a maxim
for handling anger: "When angry, count ten before you speak; if
very angry, count a hundred."[3] About seventy-five years later, Mark
Twain revised those words. His version was, "When angry, count
four; when very angry, swear."[4]

There have been a lot of remedies for anger over the years, but
perhaps we would do best to read the divine instructions given us
through Solomon.

First: *Learn to ignore petty disagreements.* Pride has a way of making
even the smallest offenses appear as unforgivable holocausts. However, Proverbs 19:11 says,

A man's discretion makes him slow to anger,
And it is his glory to overlook a transgression.

We must not forget the simple truth that "If you don't quarrel,
there won't be one." Instead of nurturing the seeds of petty offenses,
we're to leave them alone to wither and die.

3. Thomas Jefferson, in *The International Dictionary of Thoughts* (Chicago, Ill.: J. G.
Ferguson Publishing Co., 1969), p. 39.

4. Twain, in *Bartlett's*, p. 762.

Second: *Refrain from close association with anger-prone people.* Few things influence us as deeply as our friendships. Which is why Solomon warns in Proverbs 22:24–25,

> Do not associate with a man given to anger;
> Or go with a hot-tempered man,
> Lest you learn his ways,
> And find a snare for yourself.

To avoid a lifestyle of anger, we must avoid the constant company of people who are prone to anger.

Third: *Keep a close check on your tongue.* When used in anger, the tongue can strike with all the destructiveness of a lightning bolt. It can spread fires through relationships that will leave only charred memories in their wake. So Solomon tells us,

> A gentle answer turns away wrath,
> But a harsh word stirs up anger. (15:1)

If you're not willing to keep a close guard over your tongue, your soul will always be embroiled in anger.

Fourth: *Cultivate honesty in communication without letting anger build up.* There is only one way to keep anger from creating barriers in relationships, and that's through open, honest communication.

> Faithful are the wounds of a friend,
> But deceitful are the kisses of an enemy. (27:6)

Fifth: *Control your anger or it will destroy you.* Wrong motives, things not going our way, hasty reactions—these are a few of the foot soldiers of unrighteous anger that can quickly overrun our hearts. To keep this from happening, we must heed what Solomon says about people who do nothing to keep their anger in check:

> Like a city that is broken into and without walls
> Is a man who has no control over his spirit. (25:28)

Self-control is the protective wall that surrounds our hearts and keeps these sinful kinds of anger from taking over our lives.

A Final Thought

"Be angry, and yet do not sin" (Eph. 4:26). There is a righteous symmetry to this verse that needs to be reflected in the life of every Christian. Some of us are out of balance because our lives are characterized by only the first half of the command, "Be angry." Others lean totally to the other side, "Do not sin," thinking that righteous living has no place for anger. Both unrestrained anger and the denial of anger will tip the scales toward unrighteousness. There is a proper balance, however, between the two halves. It can be brought about by the exercise of our will, which stands in the gap between "Be angry" and "do not sin."

Living Insights

In our last study, we looked at several Scripture references dealing with anger. Let's look at a few of those again plus some new ones, and carry our study a step further.

- Examine the context of the following verses. Which of the passages deal with justifiable anger? Which with unjustifiable anger? Study each passage carefully; then check (✔) the appropriate box and write down why you think that particular example of anger is justified or unjustified.

Gen. 4:3–7 ☐ Justified ☐ Unjustified

_____

_____

Gen. 39:19 ☐ Justified ☐ Unjustified

_____

_____

Exod. 32:19 ☐ Justified ☐ Unjustified

_____

_____

Esther 1:12 ☐ Justified ☐ Unjustified

_____

_____

Matt. 5:21–24 ☐ Justified ☐ Unjustified

_____

_____

Gal. 5:20   ☐ Justified   ☐ Unjustified

_____

_____

Eph. 4:26   ☐ Justified   ☐ Unjustified

_____

_____

James 1:19–20   ☐ Justified   ☐ Unjustified

_____

_____

🍇 _Living Insights_   STUDY TWO

We all experience anger. The important thing is how we deal
with it. Let's take a more personal look at the principles we learned
in our lesson.

- The following five statements are the principles we studied regarding how to deal with anger. How can each be applied in
  your own life? Spend a few moments thinking through this, and
  then write out your ideas on the lines provided.

  1. Learn to ignore petty disagreements.

  _____

  _____

  _____

  _____

  2. Refrain from close association with anger-prone people.

  _____

  _____

  _____

  _____

3. Keep a close check on your tongue.

_____

_____

_____

_____

4. Cultivate honesty in communication without letting anger build up.

_____

_____

_____

_____

5. Control your anger or it will destroy you.

_____

_____

_____

_____

Chapter 9

THE PROBLEM OF LONELINESS

2 Timothy 4:9–21

Loneliness . . . it's been called the most desolate word in the English language. And we all know why.

Because we've heard the painful creak of the porch swing swaying crookedly with one-sided weight. We've woken up with the covers rumpled on just our side of the bed. We've eaten dinners for one at tables for two and stared at phones far more conspicuous in silence than they ever were in raucous ringing.

We know how loneliness feels.

And so did Paul.

Today we'll look at the emotional words of a logical man, penned from an aching heart and an empty cell. We'll read between the lines to find out where his loneliness came from and how he dealt with it.

Paul's Situation . . . Reasons for Loneliness

Second Timothy 4 leaves us the apostle Paul's last written words, and there's something in their tone that tells us he knew it. Paul had come to the end of a rich, full life, but he had come with persecution and pain—and loneliness. Let's look at some of the reasons this man of many disciples and deep fellowship with God might have experienced that kind of heartache.

His Location

It is difficult to really appreciate a passage of Scripture until you've explored the circumstances in which it was written. This last letter of Paul's wasn't written from a pastor's study or some serene hilltop. It wasn't scribbled on a camel-back journey or missionary sea crossing. It was scrawled in a dungeon, in the Mamertine Prison of Rome. One modern-day visitor to that prison wrote this about it:

> Any tourist today who leaves the guided tours and makes his own way under the brow of the Capitoline Hill in Rome will find himself admitted to a narrow,

64

dark stairway. Descending the winding stone staircase he comes finally to the dismal, dark, low-arched chamber where the apostle lay bound waiting to be offered up. Even on a hot summer day the visitor will sense the constriction of the low ceiling and the dampness of the dungeon.[1]

Not exactly the place where you'd want to spend your final days writing your memoirs.

His Relationship to Others

Paul was used to being with groups of people, ministering either to or with them. But now the only voices that echoed in his depressing stone cell were those of his guards and his faithful friend Luke. Listen to the desolation in his words to Timothy:

> Make every effort to come to me soon; for Demas, having loved this present world, has deserted me and gone to Thessalonica; Crescens has gone to Galatia, Titus to Dalmatia. Only Luke is with me. (vv. 9–11a)

The Time of Year

There's a third reason for Paul's loneliness, and that's the season of the year. Fall had quenched summer's sun with gloomy skies and chilly winds, and winter was creeping around the corner. The light that may have filtered into his cell had gone from cheering yellow to dim, rainy gray, dampening his spirits along with the sodden ground. That's the reason for his repeated plea in verse 21a: "Make every effort to come before winter."

His Future

Not only was winter near; worse, death was near. No matter how Paul may have looked forward to heaven, it would have been difficult to look forward to dying. Especially dying this way, little by little, always waiting for the final execution. It's plain from his words in verse 6 that he knew the end was near.

> For I am already being poured out as a drink offering, and the time of my departure has come.

His Thoughts

The fifth reason Paul was lonely was that he was filled with bittersweet memories that swelled his heart and touched his soul.

1. Charles C. Ryrie, "Especially the Parchments," *Bibliotheca Sacra* (January–March, 1960), p. 243.

At my first defense no one supported me, but all deserted me; may it not be counted against them. But the Lord stood with me, and strengthened me, in order that through me the proclamation might be fully accomplished, and that all the Gentiles might hear; and I was delivered out of the lion's mouth. (vv. 16–17)

Paul's Requests . . . Remedies for Loneliness

Paul had good reasons for being lonely, but unlike most of us, he didn't isolate himself and hold a private pity party. Instead, he wrote an invitation for assistance, requesting four things to sweeten his bitter circumstances.

Companionship

The first thing Paul asked for is companionship (vv. 9, 11, 21). And not just any companionship—besides Timothy, Paul specifically wanted Mark to come (v. 11).[2] Notice that Paul didn't issue a "come one, come all" invitation. He didn't instruct Timothy to share the gospel with his shipmates on the boat ride over and then bring them all to the cell for fellowship and worship. When you're really lonely, you don't want a crowd of strangers. Only your closest friends will do.

Bodily Comfort

The second thing Paul asked for was his cloak (v. 13a). Apostle or not, Paul wasn't so spiritual that he didn't feel the cold, and he wasn't so eager to die that he gave up trying to take care of himself. He *was* just human enough that he wanted his favorite garment. He didn't ask Timothy to bring him a new cloak or to borrow someone else's; he asked for a certain one that he'd left in a certain place. Listen to what Charles Ryrie has to say about Paul's request.

> Look at that cloak for a moment. It was a travelling cloak with long sleeves. Perhaps Paul had woven it himself, and it may have been over its sleeves that other cloaks had been draped when Stephen was martyred. It had a rich history in the service of Christ. It had been wet with the brine of the Agean, yellow with the dust of the Ignatian Way, white with the snows of Galatia and Pamphylia, and crimson with the blood

---

2. This is the same John Mark who, on his first missionary trip, deserted Paul in Pamphylia. He was also the reason Paul and Barnabas parted ways (Acts 15:36–40). But over time, Paul came to see Mark's strengths instead of his weaknesses, and now he realized that it was Mark who might best understand his loneliness.

of his own wounds. And now it was to serve its last purpose and keep an aged man warm during a cold winter.[3]

Reading Material

Paul next asked for his books (v. 13b). These are evidently works other than Scripture; perhaps they're the great works of literature that had helped to form his mind and his thoughts. Now, obviously, Paul wasn't planning any evangelistic tours or church services during these final days. He just wanted his books because he loved to read and he loved to learn, even in his last days on earth. Being surrounded by his books would be, to him, like being surrounded by old, dear friends.

The Scriptures

Paul's last request was predictable—along with his books, he asked for "especially the parchments" (v. 13b). By "parchments" he meant his old copies of the Scriptures. The ones with the dog-eared pages and notes in the margins, the circled words and torn covers. He wanted his old, familiar copy of the Word.

Paul's Example

Nobody escapes the isolating pangs of loneliness. And for the non-Christian, there is no method of defense. You can surround yourself with friends and immerse yourself in activity, but when you turn out the light and put your head on your pillow, you know inside that you're all alone. There is no solution to that soul-deep loneliness but the Savior.

For the Christian, that kind of loneliness has come to an end. But there still come times of feeling alone, when we long for earthly comfort. And in those times, we'll be wise to follow Paul's example and learn four practical principles for lifting our spirits and beating those blues.

Seek out some close friends.

When loneliness creeps up on us like a tide of despair, we're tempted to withdraw from people and let ourselves drown. It takes vulnerability to let people know we need them. It takes courage to ask for help. But in order for someone to come, we have to send out an invitation.

3. Ryrie, "Especially the Parchments," pp. 243–44.

Take care of your physical needs.

Loneliness has a way of draining the energy from our limbs and the taste from our food. It deadens our brains with the morphine of apathy, and we slip into neglect, letting ourselves go. One way to battle loneliness is to battle its symptoms—fight that inertia with everything you've got, and take good care of yourself.

Expand your mind with challenging books.

Reading good books will broaden your perspective and help lift you out of the doldrums. After all, there can be more to a solitary evening than sitcom reruns and the nine o'clock movie.

Get into the Word of God on a regular basis.

Returning to the Word helps you return to its Author, the One who did away with eternal loneliness when He died on the cross. His comfort may not share your table or fill your couch, but it can warm your heart and soothe your soul.

> For I am convinced that neither death, nor life, nor angels, nor principalities, nor things present, nor things to come, nor powers, nor height, nor depth, nor any other created thing, shall be able to separate us from the love of God, which is in Christ Jesus our Lord. (Rom. 8:38–39)

 Living Insights

Loneliness may enter your life from a variety of causes. It's good to know not only the reasons, but also the accompanying feelings during these painful times. Let's learn how to look for emotions by searching out David's feelings during a lonely time in his life.

- Psalm 25 gives us a window into David's lonely soul. Read this psalm slowly; then, in the following chart, write down all the emotions and feelings you find.

Psalm 25: A Look at a Lonely Man

Verse	Feelings

This study concluded with some very practical ways to help alleviate the problem of loneliness. Let's apply them to our own situations.

* Whom can you rely on for companionship when going through periods of loneliness? Jot down their names in order of availability.

  1. _____   3. _____

  2. _____   4. _____

* What are some things you can begin to do to comfort and strengthen your body? Write down an action plan.

  _____

  _____

  _____

  _____

- What books can you read to stretch your mind? Write down three or four titles from which to choose over the next few weeks.

_____

_____

_____

_____

- How can you find more intimacy with Christ through the reading of the Scriptures? Write down your ideas in the space provided.

_____

_____

_____

_____

Chapter 10

THE PROBLEM OF DOUBTFUL THINGS

1 Corinthians 8, 10

In July of 1874, the King of Cambodia was thrown from his carriage and knocked unconscious. But none of his servants dared to help him; if it weren't for the European who happened to pass by and offer to carry him to the palace, the king would be lying on that road still.

Why? Because in Cambodia, no one was allowed to touch the king for any reason without his express command. It was taboo.

A Toumbuluh man doesn't believe in tying knots; when his wife is pregnant, he refrains even from sitting with his legs crossed. He's afraid it might thwart the straightforward process of events.

The fetish priests of the Loango Coast do not eat or even look at a variety of animals and fish, although they may drink fresh blood. The head chief of the Masai is only allowed to eat milk, honey, and roasted goat livers—if he eats anything else, he might lose his magic powers. The diet of the king of Unyoro in Central Africa was even more specific. He could never eat vegetables or mutton, but lived mainly on milk and beef. And even that had to come from animals less than a year old. He could not drink milk and eat beef at the same meal, and the milk had to come from a sacred herd of exactly nine cows.[1]

All this sounds pretty bizarre to our cultured minds. Yet we Christians have a few taboos of our own, although they vary from group to group. For instance, until lately, a "good" Christian didn't drink, dance, smoke, play cards, or go to the movies, and many of these ideas still hold. Amish people don't allow their faces to be reproduced in photographs or art; some Pentecostal groups refrain from watching television or permitting women to wear pants or makeup or cut their hair. As recently as the early seventies, some Baptist groups considered it inappropriate for young boys and girls to go swimming together.

---

1. See Sir James George Frazer, *Taboo and the Perils of the Soul*, from *The Golden Bough: A Study in Magic and Religion*, 3d ed. (New York, N.Y.: Macmillan Co., 1951), pp. 226, 291–92, 298.

But where do we get these ideas? Most seem to be an attempt at clearing the fog from those "gray areas"—those tricky issues that the Bible doesn't directly address. And as long as there have been Christians, there have been disagreements as to how to handle those puzzling situations.

Take for example the early Corinthians. They had a whole slew of questions for Paul. In fact, he spent a good part of 1 Corinthians answering those questions. Let's look specifically at one of their areas of confusion and see how Paul addressed it. From his answers we can glean some principles on how to handle those gray areas we come across in our own lives.

Problems in Corinth

The Corinthian Christians were concerned about the practice of eating meat that had been sacrificed to idols. This issue was as relevant to their lives as the issue of social drinking is to ours—some were strongly against it, some felt it was perfectly all right. To better understand the situation, let's take a closer look at it.

Generally

When a sacrifice was made to an idol, only part of the meat was actually burned on the altar—a lot of steak and roast and hamburger was left over. When the idol was worshiped publicly, some of the leftover meat was given to the priests, and the rest went either to the temple butcher or the temple restaurant. In the case of private worship, the remaining meat was served at a dinner party.

Specifically

First-century Christians were faced with three sticky problems. First, there was the *restaurant* problem (1 Cor. 8:10). Should they go through the temple door and—instead of turning to the right to worship an idol or left to indulge lustful desires with the so-called priestesses—head toward the restaurant and enjoy a delicious meal? Second, there was the *meat market* problem (10:25–26). Should a Christian shop for meat at the temple market? Third, there was the problem of the *private dinner party* (v. 27). Should a believer accept an invitation from someone who would be serving food left over from a personal sacrifice?

Guidelines to Go By

In chapters 8 and 10 of 1 Corinthians, Paul offered these struggling believers some principles that are just as relevant to any cloudy issue we face today.

The Principle of Liberty

Paul's first response to the Corinthians' question was to remind them of two things they already knew.

> Now concerning things sacrificed to idols, we know that we all have knowledge. . . . Therefore concerning the eating of things sacrificed to idols, we know that there is no such thing as an idol in the world, and that there is no God but one. (8:1a, 4)

The first point Paul made was that *we know we all have knowledge.* He was referring to the knowledge of liberty. The Corinthians knew, as we know, that they no longer had to live according to a code of ethics in order to please God; that issue was taken care of on the Cross.

His second point was that *we know idols are nothing.* The believers at Corinth knew that the idols the heathen worshiped were nothing more than the wood or stone or jewels they were made of, and that sacrifices made to them had no real spiritual significance (see vv. 5–6).

Taken together, these two points let them know that there was nothing intrinsically wrong with Christians eating meat sacrificed to idols—that's the principle of liberty. But lest that principle be misapplied, Paul went on to balance it with the principle of love.

The Principle of Love

> Knowledge makes arrogant, but love edifies. (v. 1b)

Just as cement without water doesn't make a sidewalk, so knowledge without love doesn't produce godly behavior. Look at verses 7–13.

> However not all men have this knowledge; but some, being accustomed to the idol until now, eat food as if it were sacrificed to an idol; and their conscience being weak is defiled. But food will not commend us to God; we are neither the worse if we do not eat, nor the better if we do eat. But take care lest this liberty of yours somehow become a stumbling block to the weak. For if someone sees you, who have knowledge, dining in an idol's temple, will not his conscience, if he is weak, be strengthened to eat things sacrificed to idols? For through your knowledge he who is weak is ruined, the brother for whose sake Christ died. And thus, by sinning against the brethren and wounding their conscience when it is weak, you sin against Christ. Therefore, if food causes my brother to stumble, I will

never eat meat again, that I might not cause my brother to stumble.

Some of the Corinthians had been Christians so long that they had the principle of liberty down pat. They could buy a steak at the temple market, bring it home, and charcoal-broil it without a twinge of conscience. But others were just spiritual toddlers, fresh out of the background of worshiping idols, and eating that meat brought back all the memories of that time in their lives. It was beyond them how any Christian could partake of a meal so tainted with heathen practices. Paul is saying that one of the strongest evidences of maturity is not the extreme to which we exercise our liberty, but the restraints we're willing to impose on ourselves for the sake of those who are weak.

Prescription for Christians

It's not hard to think of present-day issues that parallel the Corinthians' struggle. But before we can decide whether to order that cocktail or attend that particular movie, we need to understand some of Paul's terms and answer a few questions.

Let's look at the terms first, which refer to the three types of people involved. There are the *weak:* those believers who lack knowledge and are easily offended. Though sincere in their walk, they can easily be misled. Then there are the *legalists:*[2] believers who conform to a code of behavior for the purpose of impressing others, like the Pharisees. Third are the *free:* those who know their liberty in Christ, but voluntarily restrict their behavior out of love for others and for God's glory.

And now the questions.

What should I give up?

The Bible is explicit about calling certain things sin, like adultery and drunkenness. In other areas, however, right and wrong are not spelled out, and it's those areas we need help with. But while the Bible may not give us answers, it does offer us guidelines to govern the things we should give up, guidelines we can see in the passage we've just studied.

The first is *anything that causes me to stumble and be weakened*—and here we are to let our conscience be our guide. If any activity

2. Though this term is not found in Scripture, the concept is (see Gal. 5:1–8). Nowhere in Scripture are we instructed to modify our behavior out of respect for legalists.

weakens us to sin, to us it *is* sin. The second principle is similar, but with a crucial difference: *anything which causes my brother to stumble and be weakened.* Those are the things that must not be done in public, and you'll see what they are if you keep your eyes open and your heart loving.

How can I maintain balance?

There will always be someone who objects to some aspect of our conduct; it's impossible to please everyone (compare 10:27–28). But before we decide whether to change our behavior, we should ask ourselves two questions: (1) Is the objecting person really trying to grow in the Lord, or is this person just wanting to sit on the sidelines sniping and griping? And (2) How many are going to be affected by what I do in my liberty? If we are in an area of the country or of the world where certain things are offensive to large numbers of people—or if the group we're part of objects, as a whole, to certain behaviors—we need to lay down our right to liberty.

How do I handle the legalist?

Follow Jesus' example. Without being rude, your first option is simply to ignore the legalist—just go on doing what you know to be right in God's eyes. Your second option is to take that person aside and explain where you stand scripturally.

If no one is looking, can I do as I please?

The first thing to remember is that God is always looking! But once we've considered that fact, the answer is a cautious yes—as long as it's not spelled out as being wrong, it doesn't cause offense to someone else, and it doesn't lead you into sin.

If I am in a public place and I want to enjoy something, should I?

The answer is summed up in chapter 10, verse 31: "Whether, then, you eat or drink or whatever you do, do all to the glory of God." Consider your circumstances. Are you amidst unbelievers, or even believers, who won't think anything of it? Go ahead! Or are you in the presence of a weaker brother who might object? Then let love be your guide and yield to his conscience, giving up what you would ordinarily be free to enjoy.

Perspective for the Christian

Every Christian reading this is in one of the three categories we discussed earlier . . . either you're one of the weak, one of the legalists, or one of the free. Whichever the category, wherever you are in your growth, you can benefit from a few last words of wisdom.

First: *If you seek balance, enjoy your liberty.* But keep the right attitude regarding your weaker brother.

Second: *If you are weak, keep growing!* Make a study of the freedom you have in Christ, and abandon your old rituals of trying to please God through codes and laws.

Third: *If you are a legalist, ask God to soften your heart toward Him.* Keep your critical spirit from wounding others, whether they are balanced and strong or tender and weak.

 *Living Insights* STUDY ONE

Those who are relatively new to Bible study often find it frustrating when they realize that all is not black or white. Those gray areas, however, show us the need to study further in order to establish principles.

• First Corinthians 8 is a chapter devoted to handling doubtful things. In the following exercise, we have divided the chapter into two sections. As you study this chapter, write down any observations related to the principles of liberty and love.

Principle of Liberty: 1 Corinthians 8:1–6

Verse	Observations

Principle of Love: 1 Corinthians 8:7-13

Verse	Observations

 Living Insights

This study carried principles of liberty as far as it could. It is now up to you to carry it one step further into the specific circumstances of your life. As you answer the following questions, add comments regarding specific situations you have faced or are facing today.

- Is there anything I should give up or stop doing?

_____

_____

_____

- How can I maintain balance?

_____

_____

_____

- How do I handle the legalistic person?

  _____

  _____

  _____

- What should be the limits of my freedom?

  _____

  _____

  _____

- Which type of Christian am I . . . weak, legalistic, or free? Why?

  _____

  _____

  _____

Chapter 11

THE PROBLEM OF DEFECTION

Jeremiah 2:1–19

It was a quiet house on a quiet street in Houston, Texas; quiet, because no one was there. The Lockshin family—father, mother, daughter, son—had left for the Soviet Union.

Recently filled prescription bottles still stood in bathroom cabinets on that day in 1986 when Arnold Lockshin's mother-in-law discovered the family's absence. Books on Marxism still occupied their place on bookshelves. Bicycles still leaned against the garage wall where Michael and Jennifer had hopped off after a neighborhood ride. Lauren and Arnold's wedding album was left behind too, along with the children's drawings and Arnold's old scientific publications.

It was defection, as furtive and clandestine as the Von Trapp family's breathless escape from the Nazis in *The Sound of Music* as they hid behind cathedral statues . . . as reckless as their panicked scramble over the mountains of Austria.

Only this was peacetime, not wartime. And it wasn't America's freedom that was being sought, but the Communist regime of Russia.

It's unfathomable to most Americans. As unfathomable as another kind of defection is to many Christians—defection from Jesus Christ. How, after tasting the fruits of freedom in the United States, could anyone want to eat the butterless bread of a Communist government? And likewise, how, after experiencing the freedom of Christ's love, could anyone willingly hold out their wrists to sin's shackles?

Christian defections are not usually as public as political ones, but they happen all the same. There aren't many churches or Sunday school classes that haven't experienced the defection of some of their members; perhaps even you've experienced defection in your own heart.

In our study today, let's examine this problem of defection in the Christian life and attempt to discover God's perspective on it, find out how it happens, and learn how to get a visa home once the defection has taken place.

79

An Example from Jeremiah

In spite of God's leadership, the tribe of Judah was sometimes a pretty wishy-washy lot when it came to following the Lord. At times their hearts would flame for Him, but it didn't take much for that flame to be doused and for them to forget it had ever burned. An example of this is found in a book written by Jeremiah, who was known as the weeping prophet. He spent his life mucking through the spiritual cesspool that had backed up around the stagnated spiritual lives of God's people.

Before we look at Jeremiah's prophetic warnings, let's understand the background of his book. The Jewish people had just come out of a time of revival under King Josiah, who took the throne at the age of eight, began to seek after the Lord when he was sixteen, and at age twenty, swept the land clean of all its idols (2 Chron. 34:1–7). As a result of this purge, revival came like a fresh, cool drink in the desert. But when Josiah died, the people drifted right back into their old habits. As we listen in on Jeremiah's warnings to them in Jeremiah 2, we'll catch a glimpse of how God viewed their defection.

Looking into the Past . . . God Remembers

First, God tells Jeremiah to remind the people of how things used to be. There's almost a wistfulness in His words as His thoughts roam over the memories of Judah's first flames of passion for Him.

> " 'Thus says the Lord,
>> "I remember concerning you the devotion
>>> of your youth,
>> The love of your betrothals,
>> Your following after Me in the wilder-
>>> ness,
>> Through a land not sown.
>> Israel was holy to the Lord,
>> The first of His harvest;
>> All who ate of it became guilty;
>> Evil came upon them," declares the
>>> Lord.' " (vv. 2b–3)

Looking at the Present . . . God Rebukes

In the next several verses, the mood changes as God begins to focus on the Israelites' present attitude.

> Thus says the Lord,
> "What injustice did your fathers find in Me,
> That they went far from Me

And walked after emptiness and became empty?
And they did not say, 'Where is the Lord
Who brought us up out of the land of Egypt,
Who led us through the wilderness,
Through a land of deserts and of pits,
Through a land of drought and of deep darkness,
Through a land that no one crossed
And where no man dwelt?'
And I brought you into the fruitful land,
To eat its fruit and its good things.
But you came and defiled My land,
And My inheritance you made an abomination."
(vv. 5–7)

And not only have the people defected, but their prophets and priests and politicians have followed them across the border.

"The priests did not say, 'Where is the Lord?'
And those who handle the law did not know Me;
The rulers also transgressed against Me,
And the prophets prophesied by Baal
And walked after things that did not profit." (v. 8)

Looking to the Future . . . God Reveals

As God looks into the future to the place their defection will lead them, He issues a warning to His fickle people.

"But now what are you doing on the road to Egypt,
To drink the waters of the Nile?
Or what are you doing on the road to Assyria,
To drink the waters of the Euphrates?
Your own wickedness will correct you,
And your apostasies will reprove you;
Know therefore and see that it is evil and bitter
For you to forsake the Lord your God,
And the dread of Me is not in you," declares the Lord
    God of hosts. (vv. 18–19)

"Egypt" and "Assyria" are synonyms for godlessness and evil. "You're on the wrong road—I'm trying to warn you!" God shouts. "You're headed the wrong way!" But we know from the rest of Jeremiah's book that the Lord's admonitions fell on deaf ears.

Specific Principles regarding Defection

The steps that led Israel's spiritual feet across heathen borders are the same ones every defector takes. Unlike the Lockshins' move to the Soviet Union, those steps aren't usually planned or calculated. Instead, they're taken carelessly and thoughtlessly, with little heed to the destination of the alluring path they tread. Let's look at five principles of defection that surface in Jeremiah 2.

First: *Defection does not occur suddenly.* Loyalty and love aren't usually washed away in the torrent of a sudden flash flood. Instead, they erode little by little, trickling in rivulets down to the sea of indifference as one little compromise is met by another (vv. 5–7). You may not even notice it happening.[1]

Second: *Defection most often occurs in times of blessing.* Verse 7 also shows us a second principle of defection, one that may be surprising: defection happens more easily in times of prosperity than in times of austerity. When testing comes, we are purified. But when prosperity comes, we're vulnerable.[2]

Third: *Defection flourishes under loose leadership.* Verse 8 offers us a third principle as it describes the behavior of the nation's leaders. Those leaders weren't doing their job. The prophets, who were supposed to be God's spokesmen, paid Him only mumbled lip service. The professionals who were trained to copy the Scriptures—"those who handle[d] the law"—didn't even know the Lord. They were just going through a ritual. Although they penned divine words, the words never penetrated their hearts. And the politicians made their own rules instead of following God's established code of ethics. Defection doesn't just multiply under loose leadership; it runs rampant.

Fourth: *Defection involves two specific sins: forsaking the true God and finding an empty substitute.*

> "For My people have committed two evils:
> They have forsaken Me,
> The fountain of living waters,
> To hew for themselves cisterns,
> Broken cisterns,
> That can hold no water." (v. 13)

---

1. A good example of this slow erosion of godliness is found in 2 Samuel 11, in the story of King David's adulterous affair. For all the good we know to be true of him, there was also a period of David's life when the gradual decline of his resistance to sin slid him to rock bottom in his episode with Bathsheba.

2. We can see this principle in action in the examples of David, Jonah, and Elijah. Each of these men experienced their weakest moments on the heels of their greatest triumphs. A passage that clearly displays this cycle of defection is Nehemiah 9:24–31, where we again see God's people turn their backs on Him after enjoying the richness of His blessings.

Not only do defectors abandon God; they replace Him. The tragedy is that it's tantamount to trading a diamond necklace for a strand of rhinestones.

Fifth: *Defection provides its own consequences.* Verse 19 exposes the saddest principle of all—it isn't the Lord who loses when we defect, it's us. The price of defection is painfully high, but unbelievable as it may seem, it's a price we volunteer to pay.

A Simple Remedy for Defection

Do you feel the stirrings of defection roiling the waters of your heart? That's a serious condition, but there's hope to be had.

If you are a child of God, you can never lose your citizenship in His kingdom, regardless of where you build your home. The tallest wall, the best-guarded border, the widest ocean can never keep your heavenly Father from pursuing you and wooing you to the ends of the earth (see Ps. 139:7–12). His love for you will remain constant, even through the bitter consequences of your decisions. And when you are ready to return, God's message through Jeremiah offers you passage home.

> "'Return, faithless Israel,' declares the Lord;
> 'I will not look upon you in anger.
> For I am gracious,' declares the Lord;
> 'I will not be angry forever.
> Only acknowledge your iniquity,
> That you have transgressed against the Lord your God
> And have scattered your favors to the strangers under
> every green tree,
> And you have not obeyed My voice,' declares the Lord."
> (Jer. 3:12–13)

Please. If you've played the prodigal and squandered your spiritual inheritance in a distant country, if you've taken the fast lane from the glittering of city lights to the garbage of the pigsty, please come to your senses . . . and come home to your Father. He's been there waiting for you, aching for you. All you have to do is turn your steps toward home, and He'll come running to embrace you with open arms.

Jeremiah 2 deals with the defection of a whole nation away from God, but the truths found within it are applicable to individual hearts as well.

- Sometimes the poetic language of Jeremiah's book is difficult to understand. Take some time now to put today's passage into your own words—paraphrase it for yourself. This will help clarify the text for you, and it will also bring its message to a more personal level.

Jeremiah 2:1–19

_____

_____

_____

_____

_____

_____

_____

_____

_____

_____

_____

_____

_____

_____

_____

_____

_____

Like a slow leak, defection seldom occurs overnight. Let's check our own hearts to see if defection is beginning to let the vitality out of our relationship with the Lord.

- All five of the principles of defection are listed below. Check which one seems to apply to you more than the others.

    ☐ Defection does not occur suddenly.

    ☐ Defection most often occurs in times of blessing.

    ☐ Defection flourishes under loose leadership.

    ☐ Defection involves two specific sins: forsaking the true God and finding an empty substitute.

    ☐ Defection provides its own consequences.

- Write down how you can patch that leak and keep your spiritual life from becoming flat.

_____

_____

_____

_____

_____

_____

_____

Chapter 12

THE PROBLEM OF FACING IMPOSSIBILITIES

John 6:1–14

Have you ever faced an impossible situation that chased you down with the voraciousness of a lion? And no matter where you turned, this carnivorous trouble pursued you, threatening to gobble up your faith?

Impossibilities can either drive us to God or devour us, leaving the carcass for the scavengers of depression, inferiority, and loneliness to pick apart.

But no problem can come in for the kill unless we let it. Our hope dies because we focus on the impossibility, letting it sink its teeth into the jugular vein of our faith. And the more obsessed we become with it, the more it squeezes the life out of us, until eventually we just give up: "There's no way. . . . He'll never change. . . . It's impossible."

This lesson is for those of you caught in impossibility's jaws. As we begin, let's look at three Scriptures that can help loosen its grip and give us perspective—something we lose quickly when we grapple with this kind of problem.

Some "Impossible" Scriptures

The prophet Jeremiah wrote,

> "'Ah Lord God! Behold, Thou hast made the heavens and the earth by Thy great power and by Thine outstretched arm! Nothing is too difficult for Thee.'" (Jer. 32:17)

It is difficult to capture in English the full color and emphasis of the original language of this passage. It begins with the strongest negative in the Hebrew language and states one of the greatest positives of Scripture: "Nothing is too difficult for God."

Let's look over at verse 27 in the same chapter,

> "Behold, I am the Lord, the God of all flesh; is anything too difficult for Me?"

Take whatever impossibility it is you're facing and substitute it for the word *anything*. God is asking, "Is _____ too difficult for Me?" And the implied answer, of course, is "Absolutely not!"

Now let's turn to Luke 18:27. It is perhaps the most important of our three passages because it is a verse of contrast.

> But He said, "The things impossible with men are possible with God."

Remember the story of Goliath? He was an Olympic-sized impossibility that put the whole Israelite army's faith to the test—and not one soldier among the thousands passed. In the end, it was the shepherd boy David who, using a sling and a stone as chalk, stepped to the front of the class and wrote on Goliath's forehead the lesson God wants everyone to hear: "Things that are impossible with men are possible with God."

One "Impossible" Event

Let's look at a familiar miracle that also happened to be a pop quiz on impossibilities for the disciples. It's the story of the feeding of the multitudes, and it's found in John 6.

The Setting

John's account of this miracle begins with the words, "After these things" (v. 1). So to get ourselves in tune with the context of the passage, we need to ask ourselves, After what things?

Here's the background. Jesus has chosen His disciples and sent them out for ministry on their own. According to Matthew 10, they have gone around to every village in the area preaching the gospel of the kingdom . . . and now this brood of faithlings has gathered back to Jesus, physically and emotionally worn out. Jesus knew they were tired, so He arranged an opportunity for them to get away from the crowds.

> After these things Jesus went away to the other side of the Sea of Galilee (or Tiberias). And a great multitude was following Him, because they were seeing the signs which He was performing on those who were sick. And Jesus went up on the mountain, and there He sat with His disciples. (John 6:1–3)

Imagine stretching out on a grassy mountainside, overlooking a peaceful lake, beside the Lord who sprinkled the stars and swirled the galaxies. The disciples had just begun to unwind in this incredible setting of creation and Creator, when the atmosphere suddenly changed.

> Jesus therefore lifting up His eyes, and seeing that a
> great multitude was coming to Him . . . (v. 5a)

The disciples were tired and wanted to be alone with the Lord, and here came an enormous crowd. According to verse 10, the number was about five thousand, not counting women and children. So it would be safe to say that a wave of people, eight to ten thousand strong, was washing up on the sides of this mountain. And since it was dinnertime, these people were hungry!

The disciples weren't sure what to do. Here they were in a barren place that no caterer would come near, with no food stores in sight and thousands of stomachs growling expectantly. It was an impossible situation.

The Test

But that's how Jesus wanted it. This tide of hungry people would provide a perfect opportunity for a quiz on impossibilities. And first to take the exam was Philip.

> Jesus therefore lifting up His eyes, and seeing that a
> great multitude was coming to Him, said to Philip,
> "Where are we to buy bread, that these may eat?" And
> this He was saying to test him; for He Himself knew
> what He was intending to do. (vv. 5–6)

The Lord knows the beginning and the end of every situation, and this one was no exception. The time in between is for our benefit, to teach us to focus our faith on Him. That's why He asked Philip this question.

> Philip answered Him, "Two hundred denarii worth of
> bread is not sufficient for them, for everyone to receive
> a little." (v. 7)

Have you ever had one of those conversations where the two of you were talking on completely different levels? Jesus just asked Philip *where*, and Philip answered *how much*.

To make sense of this, we need to understand Philip. He's the one who later will say to the Lord, "Just let us see God and we won't have any more questions." He was the kind of fellow who had to see everything, who seemed to have a slide rule for a mind. So he looked at their cash flow and looked at the people, and he quickly calculated in terms of bare minimums that nearly a year's earnings would not be enough. He saw the size of the problem, but was blind to the size of God.

Another disciple also took a swing at the test—Andrew. Andrew didn't wait to be called on; he raised his hand.

> One of His disciples, Andrew, Simon Peter's brother, said to Him, "There is a lad here who has five barley loaves and two fish, but what are these for so many people?" (vv. 8–9)

For a moment there, it sounded like Andrew might just ace this test, with a faith capable of believing that Christ could work a miracle with so little. If only he had stopped. But he didn't. He added the unfortunate disclaimer, "But what are these for so many people?" Andrew was a hard worker, but he was easily shot down by the prospect that the odds were against him.

The Miracle

In the curriculum of faith, the subject of impossibilities was still a grade level above the disciples' comprehension. So the Lord used an object lesson to get His point across. In a quiet, unobtrusive fashion, Jesus rang the bell for school to begin by having the disciples tell the people to sit down (v. 10). Using the Twelve as teacher's aides, Jesus got them personally involved in carrying out the miracle. Because it was for their benefit, just as much as for the benefit of the thousands.

> Jesus therefore took the loaves; and having given thanks, He distributed to those who were seated; likewise also of the fish as much as they wanted. (v. 11)

You can't fully appreciate this unless you understand that *fish* was the word used for little pickled fish, like sardines, not great big bass or salmon. And barley loaves were the size of large pancakes—flat, hard, and brittle.

Jesus took these brittle loaves and tiny fish in His hands and pulled off the impossible. And the disciples helped take that impossible food out to dozens, hundreds, even thousands of people. When they had eaten all they wanted, Jesus had the disciples gather up twelve basketfuls of leftover fragments to underscore the truth that what's impossible for men is possible for God. What had started with Philip figuring out the minimums and with Andrew looking at the odds ended with Jesus doing abundantly more than any of them could imagine. Class dismissed!

Personal Application

Mark 9 records another "impossible" situation where a man had reached the end of his rope . . . perhaps like many of us.

> "Teacher, I brought You my son, possessed with a spirit . . . And I told Your disciples to cast it out, and they could not do it." And [Jesus] answered . . . "Bring him to Me!" And they brought the boy to Him. And when he saw Him, immediately the spirit threw him into a convulsion, and falling to the ground, he began rolling about and foaming at the mouth. And He asked his father, "How long has this been happening to him?" And he said, "From childhood. And it has often thrown him both into the fire and into the water to destroy him. But if You can do anything, take pity on us and help us!" And Jesus said to him, " 'If You can!' All things are possible to him who believes." Immediately the boy's father cried out and began saying, "I do believe; help my unbelief." (vv. 17–24)

Many of us feel as though we've tried everything and are at the end of our rope, just like that father in the story. What's God saying to you right now? "All things are possible to him who worries"? No. "All things are possible to him who attempts to work it out by himself"? No. "All things are possible to him who believes."

Sometimes our worst problem is that we hold on to our problems. Look at it this way. If you had an expensive watch that stopped working, would you grab a screwdriver to break the thing open and start working on it yourself? By the time you finally gave up and took it to an expert, it would look like a bomb went off inside it.

In the same way, when we try to fix an impossible situation ourselves, we end up just making things worse. Instead, we need to take those situations to the Lord. He's the specialist when it comes to handling impossibilities.

🍇 Living Insights

Are you in a set of circumstances that seem impossible? The disciples certainly felt that way when they faced the hungry crowd on the mountainside. Let's take another look at their situation.

- The feeding of the five thousand is unique in that it is the only miracle mentioned in all four Gospels. Comparing the four accounts of the story is like looking at a statue from four different angles—each view gives you a slightly different perspective. Let's do that now with this passage. Fill in the following charts with the bits and pieces of new information you find in each retelling.

Matthew 14:13–21

New Information	Verse

Mark 6:30–44

New Information	Verse

Continued on next page

Luke 9:10–17

New Information	Verse

John 6:1–14

New Information	Verse

 Living Insights

God specializes in things we think are totally impossible. Let's use our time today to memorize a statement that will bring our seemingly impossible situations into God's perspective.

> We are all faced with a series of great opportunities brilliantly disguised as impossible situations.

Is there a situation in your life that this statement might apply to? Consider the implications that adopting this perspective might have for you.

Chapter 13

THE PROBLEM OF DEATH

Selected Scripture

Remember those special fairy tales that were like sacred texts to you as a child? The ones that helped you sort out your life, your values, helped you find your footing on that mixed plane of reality and fantasy called childhood? Most of us can probably still recall the names of our most venerated and dog-eared mentors.

To introduce us today to the problem of death, let's go back to one of those familiar classics for yet one more lesson about life.

Prinderella and the Cince

Twance upon a wine, there was a gritty little pearl named Prinderella. Prinderella had two sisty uglers and a micked wepstother who made her wean the clindows, flub the scoors, pine the shots and shans, and do all the other wirty dirk.

One day, all the gritty young pearls were invited to a drancy bess fall at the kalace of the ping. But Prinderella couldn't go—she didn't have a drancy fess, but only a rirty dag which fidn't dit. Thut ben, who should appear but Prinderella's gairy fodmother. In the eyeling of a twink, she changed a cumpkin into a poach, hice into morses, and the rirty dag into a drancy fess.

Prinderella pranced all night with the pransome young hince, but then at the moke of stridnight, she ran down the peps of the stalace and, on the bottom pep, slopped her dripper. The next day, the ping issued a kroclamation that all gelligible earls were to sly on the dripper. The sisty uglers slyed on the dripper, but it fidn't dit. Then, Prinderella slyed on the dripper, and it fid dit. So Prinderella married the hince and they hived lappily ever after.

The Cinderella you remember probably never slopped her dripper! But that's the kind of thing that can happen when you twist the words of a story—you end up with something that sounds familiar, but really is total nonsense. It's called a spoonerism. The words in the story have lost their meaning through distortion. And to someone who doesn't know the original, it wouldn't make any sense.

Like our world. A world that has been translated from its original state of paradise into something twisted, distorted, and dying.

Mixing up the words and distorting the meaning of a fairy tale like Cinderella is harmless and even amusing. But when it comes to living in a real world that's been distorted by death, that's a different story.[1]

So for the next few minutes, let's examine five basic questions concerning death through the undistorted, divine perspective found in the Scriptures.

What is death?

In order to answer this question, we first need to understand how we are made. First Thessalonians 5:23 says,

> Now may the God of peace Himself sanctify you entirely; and may your *spirit* and *soul* and *body* be preserved complete, without blame at the coming of our Lord Jesus Christ. (emphasis added)

Essentially, God created us with two parts. One is the invisible, inner part made up of the soul and the spirit, and that part is eternal. We receive it at the time of conception, and it is the seat of our personality. The second part is our body, the tangible outer shell of skin and bones that houses our soul and spirit. Death takes place when the soul and the spirit separate from the body.

One way to illustrate what happens in death is to imagine a glove on your own hand. The glove fits your hand in such a way that it looks like your hand, but it is really only a wrapping or covering. Inside this glove is your real hand. Removing the glove doesn't change anything about the hand inside it. Likewise, when we die, we are merely casting off an outer shell that isn't needed where we'll be going (see 1 Cor. 15:50).[2]

---

1. When God created the earth, He intended it to remain the paradise Adam and Eve experienced in the Garden of Eden. But when Adam sinned, he not only died spiritually and became separated from God—he also began to age, to move toward physical death. The original version of how God meant life to be was marred for all of us by Adam's sin (see Rom. 5:12).

2. All through the Bible the ideas of death and separation are used interchangeably. When death takes place, the inner man, the soul and spirit, separates instantly from the outer physical body which remains until a future resurrection. For example, when Christ was on the cross and the thief next to Him asked, "Jesus, remember me when

Does everyone die?

> Just as through one man sin entered into the world,
> and death through sin, . . . so death spread to all men,
> because all sinned. (Rom. 5:12)

The rule for all mankind is simple—all die. But even this rule has had a few exceptions ordained by God.

Two such exceptions are the Old Testament saints Enoch (see Gen. 5:21–24) and Elijah (see 2 Kings 2:11). Both of these men bypassed the experience of death and went straight into God's presence. The only other exception to death is found in 1 Corinthians 15, and it refers to those still living at the time of the Rapture.

> Behold, I tell you a mystery; we shall not all sleep, but
> we shall all be changed, in a moment, in the twinkling
> of an eye, at the last trumpet; for the trumpet will
> sound, and the dead will be raised imperishable, and
> we shall be changed. (vv. 51–52)

What happens afterward?

What will happen after death depends on what has happened before death between you and the Lord. The destiny of the person who has never trusted Christ for salvation is totally different from that of the one who has. Let's consider first what becomes of those who know the Lord Jesus.

> For we know that if the earthly tent which is our
> house is torn down, we have a building from God, a
> house not made with hands, eternal in the heavens.
> (2 Cor. 5:1)

Just as a tent is usually considered a temporary dwelling, so our physical bodies are only a temporary shelter for our soul and spirit. One day death will tear down that tattered tent, and it will be replaced by a permanent, eternal dwelling made by God.

For those who do not know the Lord Jesus, the Scriptures teach that they will pass away into a place of "torment" (see Luke 16:19–31) called "death and Hades" (see Rev. 20:13), a place of

---

You come in Your kingdom," Jesus said, "*Today* you shall be with Me in Paradise" (Luke 23:42–43, emphasis added). The body remained on the cross, while the real person went to be with the Lord in heaven. Jesus Himself, when He was ready to die, said, "Father, into Thy hands I commit My spirit" (v. 46). And with that He breathed His last, and His spirit departed, leaving His physical body behind to be embalmed and put into a tomb.

conscious, terrible anguish. And there they will remain until ultimate doom is pronounced on them at the great white throne judgment, mentioned in Revelation 20:11–15.

> And I saw a great white throne and Him who sat upon it, from whose presence earth and heaven fled away, and no place was found for them. And I saw the dead, the great and the small, standing before the throne, and books were opened; and another book was opened, which is the book of life; and the dead were judged from the things which were written in the books, according to their deeds. And the sea gave up the dead which were in it, and death and Hades gave up the dead which were in them; and they were judged, every one of them according to their deeds. And death and Hades were thrown into the lake of fire. This is the second death, the lake of fire. And if anyone's name was not found written in the book of life, he was thrown into the lake of fire.

A mistaken idea many people have is that only the Christian has eternal life. But *everyone* has eternal life—the difference is in where it's spent. Which raises another question.

How can a God of love take pleasure in tormenting people forever?

This question, however, is unanswerable, because it is full of fallacies. First, the Bible never says that God takes pleasure in tormenting people. Second, the Bible never says that God personally torments people. Instead, it's the loneliness, ache, and abandonment of hell that plagues the unbeliever through eternity. The only thing right about this question is that God *is* a God of love (see 1 John 4:7–8). But God is also perfect, pure, holy, and just (see 1 Pet. 1:15–16). So when people choose to spurn His love and go their own way, they are choosing to suffer the consequences which accompany that path. As C. S. Lewis said in *The Great Divorce,* "There are only two kinds of people in the end: those who say to God, 'Thy will be done,' and those to whom God says, in the end, 'Thy will be done.'"[3]

---

3. C. S. Lewis, *The Great Divorce* (New York, N.Y.: Macmillan Publishing Co., 1946), p. 72.

What about funerals?

As Christians, our heart's desire should be that Christ will be exalted even in our death (Phil. 1:20). So we need to give some serious thought about how this can be achieved at a funeral. Here are a few ideas to spur your own thinking.

Regarding the Funeral Service

An obvious question is whether or not to have an open casket. For all of us, there are deep emotional attachments with the earthly tent that's left behind. But does an open casket put the focus on the shell rather than the spirit and soul that have left it?

An alternative to consider is a private graveside service just for the family and, after that, a special service without the casket for friends and acquaintances. It could be a praise service—a time to worship God and remember what this person meant to those left behind.

Regarding Afterward

There are even some ways to glorify Christ after the funeral. Have you ever considered putting a statement of your faith in your will? Charles Dickens, for example, included in his will the words, "I commit my soul to the mercy of God, through our Lord and Saviour Jesus Christ."[4] Or how about sending an announcement of your loved one's death with a clear presentation of that person's testimony for Christ? One last suggestion would be to designate the money normally spent on flowers for a favorite mission, church, or special project of the deceased.

Remember, though, that these are just some suggestions which are aimed at getting away from age-old pagan practices that have filtered down to us through the years. Most of the details are a matter of personal preference.

A Concluding Thought

Trying to understand death's role in the story of the human race is a lot like trying to understand the fractured fable of Prinderella—it won't make a lot of sense unless you're familiar with the original. So it is not surprising that down through the centuries unregenerate man has come up with many different kinds of explanations concerning death.

---

4. Charles Dickens, as quoted in *Knight's Master Book of New Illustrations*, comp. Walter B. Knight (Grand Rapids, Mich.: William B. Eerdmans Publishing Co., 1956), p. 157.

Fortunately, Someone came who understood the distorted story of mankind. Someone who could tell us what the original was like, why it had changed, and how we could, through Him, overcome death.

> Jesus said to her, "I am the resurrection and the life; he who believes in Me shall live even if he dies." (John 11:25)

 ## Living Insights

We looked at many Scriptures in our lesson today, but let's study one passage a little closer, 2 Corinthians 5:1–10. These verses develop some key truths in understanding the subject of death.

- Scrutinizing the language of a passage can sometimes enhance your understanding of it. As you study these ten verses, look for key words, phrases that indicate a cause-and-effect relationship, contrasts or comparisons, repeated words or phrases, prepositions or conjunctions that connect thoughts, and statements of emphasis. Write down your discoveries in the space provided.

2 Corinthians 5:1–10

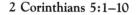

_____

_____

_____

_____

_____

_____

_____

_____

_____

_____

_____

_____

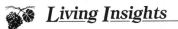 *Living Insights*

What are your perspectives and feelings about death? Do you find comfort in God's Word when it comes to this topic? Why or why not? Take this time to examine your heart, and write down what you find. Then close in prayer, asking God to meet your needs, whatever they may be.

_____

_____

_____

_____

_____

_____

_____

_____

_____

_____

_____

Chapter 14
CRUCIAL QUESTIONS CONCERNING THE DEAD
Selected Scripture

If you were to strip a young boy of his mother and sisters near a flaming pit that glowed with the charcoal of children's bodies; if you were to force him to work under the smell and curling, black smoke of burning flesh; if you were to scorch his mind with memories of hangings, beatings, shootings, electrocutions, starvations, and more, you would only be scratching the surface of Elie Wiesel's world in the Nazi death camps described in his book *Night*.

This book cracked the seal on the self-imposed, ten-year vow of silence Wiesel made before he would try to describe his passage through the valley of the shadow of death. A passage that robbed him of his feelings, his family, and his faith, leaving behind only a living corpse with torturous questions.

But Wiesel never forgot what a devout Jewish man once told him about the importance of questions: "Man raises himself toward God by the questions he asks Him."[1]

Questions are powerful enough to launch our attention heavenward, to lift our eyes off ourselves and onto Someone higher. And one of the most important questions Elie Wiesel asked—a question everyone asks—is, What about death?

In our last lesson, we began answering the questions that death forces on all of us. Questions like, What is death? Does everyone die? What happens then? Today we will be addressing six more questions that death leaves on our doorsteps.

What about suicide?

For most of us, our day will come to a close with dinner, relaxation, and comfortable sleep in our own beds. But for eighty-four other people, it will not end that way, nor will it for their friends and family. Those eighty-four will commit suicide.[2] More and more,

---

1. Elie Wiesel, *Night* (New York, N.Y.: Bantam Books, 1960), p. 2.

2. The American Association of Suicidology, "U.S. Suicide: 1986 Official Final Data."

our lives and our children's lives are being touched by this kind of death and the questions that ripple from it. Questions like, What kind of people commit suicide? Why do they do it? Is this the unpardonable sin? Let's turn to God's Word to try to find some of these answers.

The Scriptures record several cases of people who took their own lives—for example, Saul (1 Sam. 31:4), Ahithophel (2 Sam. 17:23), and Judas Iscariot (Matt. 27:3–5). From them, we can glean three important observations. First, believers as well as non-believers commit suicide. Second, excruciating circumstances often surround the person who commits suicide. Third, in the cases of Saul and Judas, there was probably some kind of satanic or demonic influence. Since Satan is both a murderer and a liar (see John 8:44), and since both Saul and Judas had been involved with Satan (see 1 Sam. 28 and John 13:21–27), it stands to reason that they could have been deluded into destroying themselves by the father of lies.

Of course, there are many other reasons why a person might choose to commit suicide—feelings of utter hopelessness, loneliness, depression, revenge, or possibly even manipulation. But regardless of the reasons, to take away a man's life is up to the One who gave it and not up to man himself (see also Ps. 139:16, 1 Cor. 6:19, and Exod. 20:13).

A question that haunts many believers is, Do people who commit suicide lose their salvation? Many have had their grief unnecessarily compounded by the unbiblical idea that suicide is the unpardonable sin. But Dr. Charles Ryrie says,

> We do know that believers do not lose their salvation because of certain kinds of sin. Admittedly suicide is a sin (for it is murder of self), but adultery and murder of someone else are also equally gross sins. Yet we know that King David, who committed both of those sins, did not lose his salvation because of it (Ro[m.] 4:7–8). The blood of Jesus Christ cleanses from all sin, including suicide.[3]

What about the death of young children?

What happens to the baby who lives only a few hours, a few months? What is the destiny of the child who dies before being able

---

3. Charles Caldwell Ryrie, *You Mean the Bible Teaches That?* (Chicago, Ill.: Moody Press, 1974), pp. 79–80.

to discern right from wrong, before reaching the age of account-ability? Let's take a look at the only case in the Bible that deals specifically with the destiny of an infant.

Second Samuel 12 is the account of God's judgment upon David for his adultery with Bathsheba. One of the heartbreaking conse-quences of David's sin was that the child of that union would die. Nevertheless, from the time the child grew ill until his death seven days later, David fasted and wept, asking God to spare the baby's life. Once that terrible week was over, however, David resumed his meals and his life—much to the amazement of his staff.

> Then his servants said to him, "What is this thing that you have done? While the child was alive, you fasted and wept; but when the child died, you arose and ate food." And he said, "While the child was still alive, I fasted and wept; for I said, 'Who knows, the Lord may be gracious to me, that the child may live.' But now he has died; why should I fast? Can I bring him back again? I shall go to him, but he will not return to me." (vv. 21–23)

David clearly identifies the destiny of this child when he says, "I shall go to him." The child was already in the presence of the Lord, where David knew he himself would go when he died.

What about cremation?

Since Scripture does not specifically address the issue of crema-tion, let's look at a few related issues and attempt to draw some con-clusions from them.

The Bible records several occasions where people were burned alive. It is called "passing through fire," and it was part of an idola-trous, pagan act (see 2 Kings 16:2–3; 21:1–2, 6).

But there is also another reason in Scripture for some people being burned, and it, too, is connected with disobedience. In these cases, God brought fire down upon individuals as a judgment (Num. 11:1, Gen. 19:24). This is not cremation, but it is interesting to note that the association of fire with the body seems to be connected with disobedience (see also Josh. 7:15–26).[4]

---

4. One exception to this seems to be the case of Saul and his sons in 1 Samuel 31:11–13. But this may have been an emergency measure to keep the Philistines from debasing the bodies, since their bones were later buried. See *The Zondervan Pictorial Encyclopedia of the Bible* (Grand Rapids, Mich.: Zondervan Publishing House, 1976), vol. 1, p. 672.

Burial seems to be the predominant method of caring for the dead throughout the Bible. For example, Abraham buried Sarah and Jacob buried Rebekah, and even when Moses died, God used the method of burial to take care of his body. Two cases of burial found in the New Testament are Lazarus and the Lord Jesus.

What about soul sleep?

The concept of soul sleep was made popular by the Seventh-Day Adventists and Jehovah's Witnesses. It is the belief that a person's soul is dormant, or asleep, from the time the body dies until the time of resurrection.

Advocates of this particular belief support their view with Bible verses that call death "sleep"—for example, Job 14:12, Daniel 12:2, and 1 Thessalonians 4:13. However, a careful study of these passages will show that in every case the word *sleep* refers only to the death of the physical body, not the soul or spirit. Luke 16:19–31, where Jesus tells the story of the rich man and Lazarus, verifies this view. At Lazarus' death the angels carried his soul to the bosom of Abraham (v. 22). The verse following the rich man's death says, "And in Hades he lifted up his eyes, being in torment" (v. 23). If his soul were asleep, he could not have been in torment.

This passage, as well as the others we considered in our last lesson under the heading "What happens afterward?" clearly teaches that if you're a Christian when you die, your soul and spirit instantly go to be with the Lord. For the non-Christian, however, the soul immediately goes to Hades, where it awaits the final judgment.

What about reincarnation?

Reincarnation—the belief that the soul or spirit returns from beyond to reinhabit another body or another form—is becoming extremely popular in our day. The Hindus, for example, teach that one spirit may be reincarnated as many as six hundred thousand times.

Those who want to embrace the Scriptures as well as a belief in reincarnation use as a proof text John 3, where Jesus tells Nicodemus that he must be born again (v. 3). They combine the idea of being born again with the last phrase in verse 8, "so is everyone who is born of the Spirit," and conclude that Jesus was teaching that the spirit can reenter life.

But the Bible makes clear that there is only one earthly existence. Hebrews 9:27 says, "It is appointed for men to die once and after this comes judgment." And Romans 6:23 says, "For the wages of sin is death, but the free gift of God is eternal life in Christ Jesus our Lord."

One other passage that makes this clear is Job 7:8–10:

"The eye of him who sees me will behold me no more;
Thine eyes will be on me, but I will not be.
When a cloud vanishes, it is gone,
So he who goes down to Sheol does not come up.
He will not return again to his house,
Nor will his place know him anymore."

We know from the context of his book that Job believed in a future resurrection, so it is obvious that he is referring here to the fact that a person dies once and does not come back to this world.

What about prayers and baptism for the dead?

Prayers for the dead are practiced in the hope of making the deceased's destiny brighter. However, there is not one verse in the Bible that teaches this. There is also not one occasion recorded where someone prayed for the dead.[5]

However, the matter of baptism for the dead is discussed in 1 Corinthians 15, the greatest chapter in the Bible concerning the resurrection of the body.

Otherwise, what will those do who are baptized for the dead? If the dead are not raised at all, why then are they baptized for them? (v. 29)

Before we simply take this verse at face value, let's examine the context of the passage a little more closely. René Pache gives us some excellent insight into what Paul is saying here.

Admission to the early Church was normally marked by the baptism of those who had believed. . . . They knew that at His return the Lord would raise again and would take unto Himself all those who had been

5. This practice has its origin in a non-canonical book called 2 Maccabees. It is one of several books that make up what is known as the apocryphal writings, books written during the four hundred years between the two testaments of the Bible. Second Maccabees tells the story of some Jewish soldiers who died in battle and how their friends prayed for them in order to help them find a better afterlife. That's where purgatory—the idea of a place where a soul could be purified after death and then pass into bliss—got its beginning. Protestants don't practice prayers for the dead because they do not believe the apocryphal books are inspired by God; they believe that these books contain contradictory and heretical teachings. Also, the Apocrypha is never quoted as inspired Scripture throughout the New Testament.

part of His Church. Now some Christians, because of illness or persecution, had not had time to be baptized. Therefore, brethren had themselves baptized in their place, so that the reception of these into the Church might be according to the rules and so that they would not risk being left behind at the resurrection.[6]

Paul does not condone this practice; he simply states it as something they were doing. Basically, he's saying, "If there's no resurrection from the dead, why bother baptizing yourselves on behalf of those who have already died?" It's not a verse about baptizing the dead, but one about the resurrection of Christians.

In Conclusion

When Elie Wiesel arrived at Birkenau, the reception center for Auschwitz, the Nazis made everyone leave their cherished possessions on the train. Then they tore family members away from one another. Then they had them strip off their clothes.

"Strip! Fast! Los! Keep only your belts and shoes in your hands. . . ."
We had to throw our clothes at one end of the barracks. There was already a great heap there. New suits and old, torn coats, rags. For us, this was the true equality: nakedness.[7]

In this ritual of death, they were stripped of everything. While the Nazis stripped their bodies, death was interrogating their souls with one ruthless question: Why live?

The apostle Paul found himself facing that same question while imprisoned in Rome. As his fate teetered between life and death, he realistically and resolutely faced his options.

For to me, to live is Christ, and to die is gain. But if I am to live on in the flesh, this will mean fruitful labor for me; and I do not know which to choose. But I am hard-pressed from both directions, having the desire to depart and be with Christ, for that is very much better; yet to remain on in the flesh is more necessary for your sake. (Phil. 1:21–24)

"To live is Christ, and to die is gain." What a clear and uncomplicated answer to death's question.

6. René Pache, *The Future Life,* trans. Helen I. Needham (Chicago, Ill.: Moody Press, 1962), pp. 90–91.

7. Wiesel, *Night,* p. 32.

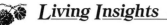

During our last two studies, we've dealt with many passages of Scripture that have shed some light on the subject of death. Hopefully, they've answered some questions and cleared up some foggy areas in your understanding of this sometimes puzzling topic. In order to solidify what you've learned, let's use this time to review Scripture passages that were especially meaningful to you.

• In the space provided, write down the references that were most helpful to you; then briefly summarize why.

Reference: _____

_____

_____

_____

Reference: _____

_____

_____

_____

Reference: _____

_____

_____

_____

Reference: _____

_____

_____

_____

Reference: _____

_____

_____

_____

In this lesson we discussed some controversial issues related to death for which many people have differing views. Where do you stand on these issues? Think through your beliefs and your reasons for them, and jot them down in the space that follows.

- Suicide: _____

  _____

  _____

- Destiny of children who die: _____

  _____

  _____

- Cremation: _____

  _____

  _____

- Soul sleep: _____

  _____

  _____

- Reincarnation: _____

  _____

  _____

- Prayer and baptism for the dead: _____

  _____

  _____

Chapter 15

THE PROBLEM OF RESENTMENT

Genesis 45:1–24, 50:15–21

All of us have felt the sting of being wrongly accused or unfairly treated. And for some of us, those barbed memories have caused a swelling of resentment.

Many of our hearts are swollen with the poison of years-old resentment because we've refused to let Christ pull the thorns. We're like small children who cry about their pain to anyone who will listen, but who won't allow anybody to touch the sore. We've chosen to respond to injustice *horizontally* rather than *vertically;* our focus is strictly on ourselves and the wrong done against us.

We do have another option, however—we can shift our focus to the vertical, choosing to set our eyes on God, not the wrong. For most of us, though, our first reaction is that it can't be done; that it sounds nice on paper, but out in the trenches of hurt feelings and ruptured relationships, it's impossible.

But somebody did it. His name was Joseph, and his story is familiar to most of us. Let's look at him again, not in the context of childhood Sunday school classes, but in the real world of ill-treatment and tough choices.

Joseph Observed

The account of Joseph's life recorded in Genesis shows that while those around him were looking at themselves or others, Joseph was looking at God. He had learned to be a vertical thinker—even when his circumstances fought to hold his attention to the horizontal.

While a Servant

In Genesis 37, Joseph is seen as the favorite son of his father. Out of jealousy, his brothers turn against him and sell him to a caravan on its way to Egypt. This is the first injustice that will trigger a whole set of others to fall like dominoes in Joseph's life.

In chapter 39, Joseph becomes the personal servant of an Egyptian official named Potiphar. But Potiphar's wife becomes attracted to Joseph, and when he will not yield to her advances, she screams accusations that he has tried to rape her. Potiphar believes his wife, and Joseph is thrown in jail.

In chapter 40, Joseph interprets a dream of Pharaoh's chief cup-bearer, who is also in prison at the time. Joseph asks him to put in a good word for him to Pharaoh when he gets out, but the cupbearer, once released, forgets him.

While a Prime Minister and Reconciling Brother

According to chapter 41, Joseph spends two more years in jail, until a miraculous event—interpreting Pharaoh's dream—not only secures his release from jail but also leads to his becoming the prime minister of Egypt. Then a famine in the land causes his brothers to come to Egypt for food (chap. 42). And what a surprise they get when they discover that the benefactor they seek is the brother they had sold into slavery years ago (45:1–3)! But despite the chain of injustices that Joseph's brothers had set off, his reaction shows his complete forgiveness.

> "And now do not be grieved or angry with yourselves, because you sold me here; for God sent me before you to preserve life. For the famine has been in the land these two years, and there are still five years in which there will be neither plowing nor harvesting. And God sent me before you to preserve for you a remnant in the earth, and to keep you alive by a great deliverance. Now, therefore, it was not you who sent me here, but God; and He has made me a father to Pharaoh and lord of all his household and ruler over all the land of Egypt." (vv. 5–8)

Joseph's focus is completely on the Lord; three times in this passage he declares that it was really God who sent him to Egypt (vv. 5, 7, 8). Instead of encountering resentment and bitterness, Joseph's brothers find that this brother they had hated has only love and compassion for them. And by his vertical response to their injustice, Joseph begins to weave the threads of a torn family back together again.

> "Hurry and go up to my father, and say to him, 'Thus says your son Joseph, "God has made me lord of all Egypt; come down to me, do not delay. And you shall live in the land of Goshen, and you shall be near me, you and your children and your children's children and your flocks and your herds and all that you have. There I will also provide for you, for there are still five years

of famine to come, lest you and your household and all that you have be impoverished."'"... Then he fell on his brother Benjamin's neck and wept; and Benjamin wept on his neck. And he kissed all his brothers and wept on them, and afterward his brothers talked with him. (vv. 9–11, 14–15)

The Scriptures don't say how long they talked or what they talked about, but there can be little doubt that the centerpiece of their conversation was Joseph's amazing attitude.

Now, we may tend to think that Joseph's head was in the clouds —that he didn't really see his brothers for what they were. But in verses 22–24, we see just how realistic Joseph was.

To each of them he gave changes of garments, but to Benjamin he gave three hundred pieces of silver and five changes of garments. And to his father he sent as follows: ten donkeys loaded with the best things of Egypt, and ten female donkeys loaded with grain and bread and sustenance for his father on the journey. So he sent his brothers away, and as they departed, he said to them, "Do not quarrel on the journey."

Who else but a brother would give a farewell like that? Joseph knew his own brothers well enough to realize they were likely to argue over what belonged to whom and end up all out of sorts.

Several years later, Joseph's father Jacob dies. For all Joseph's kindness toward them, the brothers begin to feel apprehensive.

When Joseph's brothers saw that their father was dead, they said, "What if Joseph should bear a grudge against us and pay us back in full for all the wrong which we did to him!" (50:15)

Suddenly, the brothers begin to wonder whether Joseph's attitude was more for the benefit of his beloved father than an act of genuine forgiveness. So, playing on Joseph's devotion to his father, they write a letter to ensure his continued goodwill.

So they sent a message to Joseph, saying, "Your father charged before he died, saying, 'Thus you shall say to Joseph, "Please forgive, I beg you, the transgression of your brothers and their sin, for they did you wrong."' And now, please forgive the transgression of the servants of the God of your father." And Joseph wept when they spoke to him. Then his brothers also came and fell down before him and said, "Behold, we are your servants." (vv. 16–18)

With this letter, Joseph is faced with another situation that could lead to bitterness. For some years now he has provided his brothers with nothing but the best, and now they are doubting his sincerity. He could have resented their lack of trust. But he responds with compassion and understanding:

> "Do not be afraid, for am I in God's place? And as for you, you meant evil against me, but God meant it for good in order to bring about this present result, to preserve many people alive. So therefore, do not be afraid; I will provide for you and your little ones." So he comforted them and spoke kindly to them. (vv. 19b–21)

Lessons Observed

Joseph is a shining example of how to respond to injustice. Let's take a moment now to look at five ways we, too, can pull the thorn of resentment out of those unjustified wrongs that will inevitably come our way.

First: *Accept your situation as being directly from the Lord.* This is a critical first step that starts the ball rolling in the right direction. If you can trust God to use even the unjust experiences of your life, you'll be on the way to gaining His perspective.

Second: *Think offensively, not defensively.* You cannot help but be jolted when a close friend or relative turns against you. That's understandable. What you have to guard against is that natural tendency to become defensive. When all your energy is focused on coming up with reasons why you don't deserve such treatment, you can't see anything but horizontal viewpoint. Offensive thinking is seeking God's strength to forgive, not gathering your own forces for a counterattack.

Third: *Consider the other person's viewpoint.* Do your best to put yourself in the other person's shoes. You may discover that some of their behavior is well-founded; if so, seek forgiveness. But even if it isn't, you may gain some insight that will open your heart to compassion.

Fourth: *Stay positive and search for God's lessons.* It's easy to let bitter circumstances sour our lives, to give in to our own negative reactions, critical spirit, and joyless countenance. We can't always be happy—our experiences in life will see to that. But there's a big difference between being happy and having joy. Joy is possible because God is always involved in our lives—it has nothing whatever to do with our circumstances.

Fifth: *Discover ways of showing kindness to the other person.* Like it or not, you're going to spend eternity with some of these folks that do you wrong here on earth! But before you groan too loudly, remember that all of us have behaved unfairly at times—so none of us should be casting any self-righteous stones. This principle is not meant to recommend the vindictive kind of advice that you hear so often, "Kill them with kindness." We are to offer a friendship that is absolutely genuine.

A Final Observation

Some Christians can give you chapter and verse on every hurt they've ever experienced. Their whole world is jaundiced with bitterness and resentment, and they become increasingly negative, critical, easily offended, and friendless. That's the exact opposite of what a Christian's life should look like.

The vertical focus that can keep resentment from corrupting our lives is mapped out for us all in the great commandment recorded in Matthew 22:37–39. It begins, "You shall love the Lord your God," which gives us our focus, our source of strength, for accomplishing the second half of the command, "[and] your neighbor as yourself."

Alexander Pope once said, "To err is human, to forgive divine."[1] By keeping his focus on God, Joseph was divinely empowered to forgive, and his world was anointed with love. Which world will you choose, one filled with resentment, or one permeated with love?

---

1. Alexander Pope, in *Bartlett's Familiar Quotations*, 15th ed., rev. and enl., ed. Emily Morison Beck (Boston, Mass.: Little, Brown and Co., 1980), p. 333.

Living Insights   STUDY ONE

The ability to see things with a vertical perspective is an attribute worth developing. Sometimes we are so horizontally oriented that we miss the lesson God is trying to teach us.

- Listed below are five men from Scripture. Based on what you know about each man, place a check (✔) by the type of perspective he most often demonstrated: vertical or horizontal. Then briefly write the reasons for your choice.

Noah   ☐ Horizontal   ☐ Vertical

_____

_____

Joshua   ☐ Horizontal   ☐ Vertical

_____

_____

Saul   ☐ Horizontal   ☐ Vertical

_____

_____

Jonah   ☐ Horizontal   ☐ Vertical

_____

_____

John the Baptist   ☐ Horizontal   ☐ Vertical

_____

_____

Living Insights   STUDY TWO

How have you handled bitterness and resentment in the past? Have you had victory over it, or has it consumed you? Let's use our time together to reflect on this.

- Is there a particular injustice you're having to face? If you are responding horizontally, what principles from this lesson do you

113

need to apply? Use the following questions to form a strategy for conquering resentment.

1. Am I seeing this experience from a vertical perspective or a horizontal one?

2. Do I see this as directly from the Lord?

3. Am I seeking God's strength?

4. Have I considered others' viewpoints?

5. Am I staying positive?

6. Do I search for God's lessons?

7. Have I discovered ways to show kindness to the other person?

Chapter 16

THE PROBLEM OF DISCOURAGEMENT

Nehemiah 4:9–23

A mother of eight children came home one day to find her youngest five huddled intently in the middle of the floor. She walked over to see what the center of attraction was and discovered they were playing with five baby skunks. Aghast, she shouted, "Run, children, run!" And run the children did—each clutching one terrified skunk![1]

Can you imagine five kids with skunks, all running in different directions? And the farther each child ran, the louder the mother probably shouted, causing all five to panic and squeeze their skunk . . . and skunks don't like to be squeezed!

All of us have had a problem blow up in our face and end up as a stinking mess. Those situations can knock the wind right out of our confidence and leave us feeling flat and discouraged. And there is nothing quite like dealing with the problem of discouragement when you're in a position of leadership—even if it's only leading five gamy children to a backyard hose.

Nehemiah found this out when he took on a seemingly uncomplicated task that turned into a sizable problem. He set out to build a wall, but he found himself climbing over sarcasm, mockery, criticism, and conspiracy. Now that's discouraging! Let's take a closer look at the problem and see what caused the discouragement and how Nehemiah dealt with it.

Causes of Discouragement

Since 586 B.C., when the Babylonians conquered the southern kingdom of Judah and took the people into exile, Jerusalem's walls had been in disarray. Now, 142 years later, Judah was beginning to dust herself off after her great spiritual fall and start walking with God again. And God wanted Nehemiah to oversee the task of rebuilding the wall around the city.

---

1. John Haggai, *How to Win Over Worry* (Eugene, Oreg.: Harvest House Publishers, 1987), p. 184.

While Nehemiah's workers were building up Jerusalem's broken walls a little more each day . . . their confidence and faith were being torn down, brick by brick, by the repeated threats and criticisms of their enemies. Finally, discouragement brought their work to a standstill. Nehemiah 4:10–11 gives us the reasons why.

> Thus in Judah it was said,
>   "The strength of the burden bearers is
>   failing,
>   Yet there is much rubbish;
>   And we ourselves are unable
>   To rebuild the wall."
> And our enemies said, "They will not know or see until we come among them, kill them, and put a stop to the work."

Loss of Strength

The very first thing this passage mentions is that the people were burned out physically; the original text says they were "stumbling, tottering, staggering under the load." One of the main reasons for rebuilding the wall was for protection. But in their haste, they had neglected to protect themselves from enemies within—exhaustion and discouragement. They had started strong, but they were too tired to finish.

Loss of Vision

The Hebrew word for *rubbish* means "dry earth, debris." The people were tired; they had done a lot of work . . . but instead of being encouraged to go on by what they had already accomplished, they saw only the huge task before them and couldn't imagine the wall ever being completed.

Loss of Confidence

The end of verse 10 shows that the erosion of the people's physical reserves and vision had also worn down their confidence. At one time the people "had a mind to work" (see v. 6). Now, their motivation was gone, and in its place was an overwhelming feeling that they could never finish the task.

Loss of Security

The Jews had enemies who didn't want to see them rebuild that wall—and they didn't keep their objections a secret (v. 11). The people had to place each brick while looking over their shoulder, not knowing from moment to moment whether they might be attacked.

Nehemiah's Cure for Discouragement

Nehemiah must have felt somewhat like that mother with the baby skunks—out of control and with a mess on his hands. The troops were wilting with discouragement and his grand idea of rebuilding the wall was crumbling before his eyes. But Nehemiah didn't stand with his head in his hands. Instead, he began putting into action five things which would rebuild the people's confidence.

He unified the people around the same goal.

> Then I stationed men in the lowest parts of the space behind the wall, the exposed places, and I stationed the people in families with their swords, spears, and bows. (v. 13)

Nehemiah saw that the basic unit of encouragement, the family, had been broken up by having relatives work at different places on the wall. He also saw that scattering the work was counterproductive. So he reorganized the work and teamed up his people into family units centered around common goals.

He directed their attention to the Lord.

> When I saw their fear, I rose and spoke to the nobles, the officials, and the rest of the people: "Do not be afraid of them; remember the Lord who is great and awesome." (v. 14a)

Nehemiah saw his people's fear and knew that he had to get their eyes back on the Lord. Their focus was on the debris and the enemy, and until that changed, there would be no progress.[2]

He encouraged them to maintain a balance.

> And it happened when our enemies heard that it was known to us, and that God had frustrated their plan, then all of us returned to the wall, each one to his work. . . . Those who were rebuilding the wall and those who carried burdens took their load with one hand doing the work and the other holding a weapon. (vv. 15, 17)

When we're discouraged, it's easy to get caught in the swings of the pendulum—to see only one view at a time, never the whole

---

2. During times of discouragement, it's important for all of us to refocus our attention on the Lord. We can do this by meditating on His promises, memorizing His Word, and reflecting on His character (see Ps. 46:10).

picture. Nehemiah probably had some workers who wanted to concentrate on building the protective wall, and others who wanted to grab their spears and go to war. He had to bring the people into a balance of continuing the work while also being prepared to fight.

He provided a rallying point.

> And I said to the nobles, the officials, and the rest of the people, "The work is great and extensive, and we are separated on the wall far from one another. At whatever place you hear the sound of the trumpet, rally to us there. Our God will fight for us." (vv. 19–20)

First of all, the rallying point involved a place. Nehemiah knew the enemy could attack at any time, in any place. The people needed to know that if one section of the wall was put under siege, the others would rally to their aid and not leave them to fight alone. Second, the rallying point involved a principle. Nehemiah bolstered his people's faith in God by reminding them that He would be fighting alongside them.[3]

He occupied them in a ministry of service to others.

> So we carried on the work with half of them holding spears from dawn until the stars appeared. At that time I also said to the people, "Let each man with his servant spend the night within Jerusalem so that they may be a guard for us by night and a laborer by day." (vv. 21–22)

Lastly, Nehemiah created a protective buddy system. He knew that if the people got involved serving one another that their confidence and morale about the project would increase, and they would be better protected from their enemies.

Our Response Today

Many of us started our Christian walk with confidence and faith —we were like the fellow Tim Hansel describes in *Eating Problems for Breakfast:* "He was the sort of man who would go after Moby

---

3. Too often, when Christians come under discouragement's attack, they have no friends to recall them to a rallying point. But the idea of drawing together, both for earthly encouragement and to be reminded of the Lord's presence, is woven throughout Scripture. When David was pursued by King Saul, Jonathan was there to encourage and help David. When Elijah was depressed and fleeing from the murderous Queen Jezebel, God sent Elisha to encourage him. We all need someone who will drop what they are doing and come running when we need help.

Dick with a row boat, a harpoon, and a jar of tartar sauce."[4] But it doesn't take long to start feeling discouraged, for some of the very same reasons as Nehemiah's crew.

Are you facing the halfway mark in some task in your world? Whether you're halfway finished building a wall or halfway through paying off a debt, discouragement may catch you unawares as you lean on your shovel to rest.

Are you overwhelmed by the task left before you? Whether you are knee-deep in crumbled bricks or desk-deep in memos and meetings, the debris of the daily routine can clutter your mind and keep you from seeing the work you've already accomplished.

Has the building up of your faith left you worn out? Have you lost your vision, your confidence? Are you feeling insecure about whether God is really going to help you when those problems attack you from all sides?

Discouragement has a strong, relentless power to pull the focus of our hearts and minds in on ourselves. It can quell our hunger for knowing and trusting in Christ and lead us to trust in our own abilities. But don't let it. Follow Nehemiah's guidelines for encouragement, and resume your task with renewed spirit.

Living Insights STUDY ONE

"He was the sort of man who would go after Moby Dick with a row boat, a harpoon, and a jar of tartar sauce."

For the next few moments, let the following questions guide you in applying some tartar sauce to one of your own discouraging problems.

• What particular area are you feeling most discouraged in?

• What is feeding that discouragement?

    A lack of strength?

    A lack of vision?

---

4. Tim Hansel, *Eating Problems for Breakfast* (Dallas, Tex.: Word Publishing, 1988), p. 22.

A lack of confidence?

A lack of security?

A lack of something else?

_____

_____

_____

- How do you respond to discouragement? What or whom do you depend on, other than God, for relieving your discouragement?

_____

_____

- What is it that you are expecting God to do before you can stop feeling discouraged?

_____

_____

- What is it that you can do—*need* to do—to nourish your faith and hope and to shrivel up your discouragement?

_____

_____

_____

 Living Insights   STUDY TWO

This series has addressed some vital concerns. As we conclude, let's look back and recall some of the insights we found most helpful.

- Begin by writing down the lessons that were most relevant to you; then, in the space provided, summarize what you plan to apply.

    Title: _____

_____

_____

_____

Title: _____

_____

_____

_____

Title: _____

_____

_____

_____

Title: _____

_____

_____

_____

Title: _____

_____

_____

_____

Title: _____

_____

_____

_____

Title: _____

_____

_____

_____

BOOKS FOR
PROBING FURTHER

As we finish this study on problems, it would be nice if we could now say, "and we lived happily ever after." But that line will come true only in eternity; it will never happen while we live in a world yoked with sin. Problems are a fact of life.

Dr. Larry Crabb, in his book *Inside Out*, makes the sad observation that "very few older [people] face their lives realistically and still cling passionately to Christ. Most are either realistic and disillusioned or believing and defensive."[1] The goal for this study has not been to provide pat answers for difficult problems, but rather to show us how to respond to Christ in the midst of problems. Hopefully, as a result, our problems will increase our passion for Him, not extinguish it.

The following books will provide you with more insights to help keep your flame alive while going through many of the problems we have touched on.

Augsburger, David. *The Freedom of Forgiveness.* Chicago, Ill.: Moody Press, 1988. The author combines personal testimonies with Scripture for a highly motivating guide to applying forgiveness in your life.

Bayly, Joseph. *The Last Thing We Talk About.* Revised edition. Elgin, Ill.: David C. Cook Publishing Co., 1973. Death is not something we want to talk about. Yet Bayly manages to do it in both a compelling and concise way in this short but poignant book.

Crabb, Larry. *Effective Biblical Counseling.* Grand Rapids, Mich.: Zondervan Publishing House, 1977. This practical book is designed to equip laypeople in effectively ministering to hurting people in the local church. It provides excellent biblical insights into personal needs, the goal of counseling, basic strategy, and a myriad of other helpful topics.

———. *Inside Out.* Colorado Springs, Colo.: NavPress, 1988. Dr. Crabb challenges us to take off our picture-perfect masks of pretension and face the inner problems that sidetrack us from truly living for God.

1. Larry Crabb, *Inside Out* (Colorado Springs, Colo.: NavPress, 1988), p. 11.

Dobson, James. *Hide or Seek*. Revised edition. Old Tappan, N.J.: Fleming H. Revell Co., 1979. Dr. Dobson has written a warm and understanding book designed especially for parents who want to guard their children against feelings of inferiority.

Hansel, Tim. *Eating Problems for Breakfast*. Dallas, Tex.: Word Publishing, 1988. More than just a guide about one particular problem, this book provides creative and accurate ways to learn how to resolve all kinds of problems that will inevitably cross our paths.

Ketterman, Grace, M.D. *Depression Hits Every Family*. Nashville, Tenn.: Thomas Nelson Publishers, Oliver-Nelson Books, 1988. Dr. Ketterman talks about how depression manifests itself in the different stages of life, discusses its contributing factors, and offers some sound, preventative advice.

Minirth, Frank B., and Paul D. Meier. *Happiness Is a Choice*. Grand Rapids, Mich.: Baker Book House, 1978. The authors combine their professional training, counseling experience, and biblical knowledge to provide a very perceptive overview on depression and its prevention.

Osborne, Cecil. *The Art of Understanding Yourself*. Grand Rapids, Mich.: Zondervan Publishing House, 1967. Osborne examines the invisible barriers that keep us from knowing and loving one another.

Swindoll, Charles R. *Encourage Me*. Portland, Oreg.: Multnomah Press, 1982. Chuck Swindoll writes to those whose hearts are thirsty for encouragement. Each chapter is written to offer an oasis for spirits that have been battered by disappointment.

———. *Three Steps Forward, Two Steps Back*. Nashville, Tenn.: Thomas Nelson Publishers, 1980. In addressing the other side of the tracks in our Christian life, Chuck looks at the side that contains the difficult problems and disappointments. In a down-to-earth way, he confronts reality and its hurts and then holds out hope for those who learn to persevere.

Yancey, Philip. *Disappointment with God*. Grand Rapids, Mich.: Zondervan Publishing House, 1988. Yancey deals insightfully with the questions that nag all of us during times of personal crisis: Is God unfair? Is God silent? Is God hidden? You will find this a sensitive, encouraging book.

Insight for Living
Cassette Tapes
YOU AND YOUR PROBLEMS

The person who says, "Accept Christ and all your problems will end," didn't get that idea from the Bible! All people have problems, including Christians. But there *are* ways to handle them. This study is filled with relevant and practical advice—all from Scripture—on facing some of the most common struggles in life. This is straightforward teaching that's easily understood.

			U.S.	Canada
YYP	CS	Cassette series—includes album cover ..	$44.50	$56.50
		Individual cassettes—include messages A and B	5.00	6.35

These prices are subject to change without notice.

YYP 1-A: *Wisdom: An Essential in Handling Problems*—
Proverbs 1:1–7, 20–32
   B: *The Problem of Inferiority*—Selected Scripture

YYP 2-A: *The Problem of the Clergy-Laity Gap*—
1 Thessalonians 2:1–12
   B: *The Problem of Temptation*—James 1:13–15

YYP 3-A: *The Problem of Depression*—Selected Scripture
   B: *The Problem of Worry*—Matthew 6:25–34

YYP 4-A: *The Problem of Anger*—Ephesians 4:26–27
   B: *A Cool Hand on a Hot Head*—Selected Proverbs

YYP 5-A: *The Problem of Loneliness*—2 Timothy 4:9–21
   B: *The Problem of Doubtful Things*—
1 Corinthians 8, 10

YYP 6-A: *The Problem of Defection*—Jeremiah 2:1–19
   B: *The Problem of Facing Impossibilities*—John 6:1–14

YYP 7-A: *The Problem of Death*—Selected Scripture
   B: *Crucial Questions Concerning the Dead*—
Selected Scripture

YYP 8-A: *The Problem of Resentment*—Genesis 45:1–24,
50:15–21
   B: *The Problem of Discouragement*—Nehemiah 4:9–23

How to Order by Mail

Simply mark on the order form whether you want the series or individual tapes. Mail the form with your payment to the appropriate address listed below. We will process your order as promptly as we can.

United States: Mail your order to the Sales Department at Insight for Living, Post Office Box 4444, Fullerton, California 92634. If you wish your order to be shipped first-class for faster delivery, add 10 percent of the total order amount (not including California sales tax). Otherwise, please allow four to six weeks for delivery by fourth-class mail. We accept personal checks, money orders, Visa, or MasterCard in payment for materials. Unfortunately, we are unable to offer invoicing or COD orders.

Canada: Mail your order to Insight for Living Ministries, Post Office Box 2510, Vancouver, British Columbia V6B 3W7. Please add 7 percent of your total order for first-class postage and allow approximately four weeks for delivery. Our listeners in British Columbia must also add a 6 percent sales tax to the total of all tape orders (not including postage). We accept personal checks, money orders, Visa, or MasterCard in payment for materials. Unfortunately, we are unable to offer invoicing or COD orders.

Australia, New Zealand, or Papua New Guinea: Mail your order to Insight for Living, Inc., GPO Box 2823 EE, Melbourne, Victoria 3001, Australia. Please allow six to ten weeks for delivery by surface mail. If you would like your order sent airmail, the delivery time may be reduced. Whether you choose surface or airmail, postage costs must be added to the amount of purchase and included with your order. Please use the chart that follows to determine correct postage. Due to fluctuating currency rates, we can accept only personal checks made payable in U.S. funds, international money orders, Visa, or MasterCard in payment for materials.

Overseas: Other overseas residents should contact our U.S. office. Please allow six to ten weeks for delivery by surface mail. If you would like your order sent airmail, the delivery time may be reduced. Whether you choose surface or airmail, postage costs must be added to the amount of purchase and included with your order. Please use the chart that follows to determine correct postage. Due to fluctuating currency rates, we can accept only personal checks made payable in U.S. funds, international money orders, Visa, or MasterCard in payment for materials.

Type of Postage	Postage Cost
Surface	10% of total order
Airmail	25% of total order

For Faster Service, Order by Telephone

To purchase using Visa or MasterCard, you are welcome to use our **toll-free** numbers between the hours of 8:30 A.M. and 4:00 P.M., Pacific time, Monday through Friday. The number to call from anywhere in the United States is **1-800-772-8888.** To order from Canada, call our Vancouver office at **1-800-663-7639.** Vancouver residents should call (604) 272-5811. Telephone orders from overseas are handled through our Sales Department at (714) 870-9161. We are unable to accept collect calls.

Our Guarantee

Our cassettes are guaranteed for ninety days against faulty performance or breakage due to a defect in the tape. For best results, please be sure your tape recorder is in good operating condition and is cleaned regularly.

Note: To cover processing and handling, there is a $10 fee for *any* returned check.

Order Form

YYP CS represents the entire *You and Your Problems* series, while YYP 1–8 are the individual tapes included in the series.

Series or Tape	Unit Price U.S.	Unit Price Canada	Quantity	Amount
YYP CS	$44.50	$56.50		$
YYP 1	5.00	6.35		
YYP 2	5.00	6.35		
YYP 3	5.00	6.35		
YYP 4	5.00	6.35		
YYP 5	5.00	6.35		
YYP 6	5.00	6.35		
YYP 7	5.00	6.35		
YYP 8	5.00	6.35		
Subtotal				
Sales tax 6% for orders delivered in California or British Columbia				
Postage 7% in Canada; overseas residents, see "How to Order by Mail"				
10% optional first-class shipping and handling U.S. residents only				
Gift to Insight for Living Tax-deductible in the U.S. and Canada				
Total amount due Please do not send cash.				$

If there is a balance: ☐ apply it as a donation ☐ please refund

Form of payment:

☐ Check or money order made payable to Insight for Living

☐ Credit card (circle one):   Visa   MasterCard

 Card Number _____ Expiration Date _____

 Signature _____
   <small>We cannot process your credit card purchase without your signature.</small>

Name _____

Address _____

City _____

State/Province_____ Zip/Postal Code _____

Country _____

Telephone _(___)_____ Radio Station ___ ___ ___ ___
   <small>If questions arise concerning your order, we may need to contact you.</small>

Mail this order form to the Sales Department at one of these addresses:
Insight for Living, Post Office Box 4444, Fullerton, CA 92634
Insight for Living Ministries, Post Office Box 2510, Vancouver, BC, Canada V6B 3W7
Insight for Living, Inc., GPO Box 2823 EE, Melbourne, VIC 3001, Australia

Order Form

YYP CS represents the entire *You and Your Problems* series, while YYP 1–8 are the individual tapes included in the series.

Series or Tape	Unit Price U.S.	Canada	Quantity	Amount
YYP CS	$44.50	$56.50		$
YYP 1	5.00	6.35		
YYP 2	5.00	6.35		
YYP 3	5.00	6.35		
YYP 4	5.00	6.35		
YYP 5	5.00	6.35		
YYP 6	5.00	6.35		
YYP 7	5.00	6.35		
YYP 8	5.00	6.35		
			Subtotal	
			Sales tax 6% for orders delivered in California or British Columbia	
			Postage 7% in Canada; overseas residents, see "How to Order by Mail"	
			10% optional first-class shipping and handling U.S. residents only	
			Gift to Insight for Living Tax-deductible in the U.S. and Canada	
			Total amount due Please do not send cash.	$

If there is a balance: ☐ apply it as a donation ☐ please refund

Form of payment:

☐ Check or money order made payable to Insight for Living

☐ Credit card (circle one):　　Visa　　MasterCard

　　Card Number _____ Expiration Date _____

　　Signature _____
　　　　　　We cannot process your credit card purchase without your signature.

Name _____

Address _____

City _____

State/Province_____ Zip/Postal Code _____

Country _____

Telephone _(_____)_____ Radio Station ___ ___ ___ ___
　　　　If questions arise concerning your order, we may need to contact you.

Mail this order form to the Sales Department at one of these addresses:
Insight for Living, Post Office Box 4444, Fullerton, CA 92634
Insight for Living Ministries, Post Office Box 2510, Vancouver, BC, Canada V6B 3W7
Insight for Living, Inc., GPO Box 2823 EE, Melbourne, VIC 3001, Australia